TRIVIATA

A Compendium
of Useless Information

TRIVIATA

A Compendium
of Useless Information

TIMOTHY T. FULLERTON

Cartoon illustrations by Harold Montiel

HART PUBLISHING COMPANY, INC.
NEW YORK CITY

DURING THE 12TH CENTURY, Sutoku, Emperor of Japan, spent a three-year exile copying the *Lankauarn Sutra*—a Buddhist religious work containing 10,500 words—in his own blood.

Topsy Turvy

On October 18, 1961, an abstract painting by Henri Matisse entitled *Le Bateau* was inadvertently hung upside down in the Museum of Modern Art in New York. The mistake went unnoticed for 47 days, during which time more than 100,000 people viewed the painting, apparently without noticing the error.

THE ICELANDIC LANGUAGE has remained unchanged since the 12th century.

THE KEENEST SENSE of smell exhibited in all nature is that of the male silkworm moth. It can detect the sex signals of a female 6.8 miles away!

AN ENGLISH HIGHWAY that runs from London to Exeter boasts the smallest underpass in the world—a tunnel one foot wide which was constructed to permit badgers to get safely to the other side of the road.

There's One Born Every Minute

In the summer of 1824, two retired New Yorkers, named Lozier and DeVoe, perpetrated a wild hoax on their numerous friends. They convinced a crowd that they had obtained the mayor's approval to saw off Manhattan from the mainland, and *turn the island around!*

The purpose of this grand plan was to keep Manhattan's southern end from sinking into the harbor under the weight of the many new buildings. DeVoe and Lozier started immediately to sign up laborers, and to award contracts for food, equipment, and even for a huge anchor to prevent the island from being swept out to sea. After eight weeks of preparation, all those associated with the project were instructed to meet the following Monday morning so they could proceed to the north end of Manhattan where the work was to begin. As instructed, hundreds of workmen plus scores of contractors arrived at the spot. They waited for hours before they learned that Lozier and DeVoe had, for reasons of health, gone on an extended journey.

GOURMETS WHO SAVOR "authentic" Chinese food may be disheartened to learn that when chop suey was first concocted in New York in 1896, the dish was completely unknown in China. A chef of the Chinese Ambassador Li Hung-Chang devised the dish to appeal to both American and Oriental tastes.

A FEW YEARS BACK a woman in Texas loved her dog so much she married him in a standard religious ceremony presided over by a cleric.

RAG APPLE, A HOLSTEIN BULL belonging to the New York Artificial Breeders Cooperative, is said to have sired over 15,000 offspring in the three years and four months of his service—an average of 87 a week.

AMONG MAMMALS, only men and monkeys are capable of distinguishing colors.

The Best-kept Secret

Since the invention of Coca-Cola, only seven men have ever known the formula for the drink. Today only two are living, and as a precaution these two men never fly in the same airplane.

Incidentally, 90 million bottles of Coke are drunk each day throughout the world.

FROM INDIA, NUTMEGS and cloves, native to the Moluccas—the Spice Islands—were introduced into China. A tradition has come down to us that in the 3rd century B. C., the courtiers of the royal court were required to carry cloves in their mouths in order to sweeten their breath when addressing the emperor.

Two WORDS in the English language contain the vowels *a, e, i, o, u*, in that order: *abstemious* and *facetious*.

ASSUMING THAT the earth were completely dry, a man walking day and night at a steady pace could circumnavigate the planet in a little less than a year. A tidal wave could accomplish a round trip in just 60 hours; a bullet, in 14 hours; and a beam of light in just one-tenth of a second.

An Enlightening Account

Man is not a nocturnal creature; his eyes do not adjust to darkness as well as do those of an owl. When early man discovered the secret of fire, he soon thereafter discovered how to brighten his night with a torch or a candle.

The candle probably evolved when a piece of wood, or rush, or cord fell into ignited fat. How astounding it must have been to realize that the foreign body was not immediately consumed.

In the late 18th and early 19th centuries, candles were made of tallow, beeswax, and vegetable wax, such as bayberry. During the past decade, there has been a great revival in candlemaking, especially of the organically scented varieties.

The first lamp was probably a dish which contained oil and a wick. The next development, thought to have originated in Egypt, was the float-wick lamp; here the wick was supported *above* the oil.

IN CASE YOU'VE FORGOTTEN: Snow White's seven dwarf friends were named Dopey, Grumpy, Sleepy, Happy, Bashful, Sneezy, and Doc.

YOU COMPLAIN THAT you never go anywhere? Well, many small rodents live out their entire existence without ever straying more than 20 feet from the place of their birth. On the other hand, a humpback whale often covers more than 4,000 miles in a single year.

A Car in Every Garage

Preceding Henry Ford by two years, Ransom Olds commercially produced a three-horsepower Oldsmobile. He produced over 400 cars a year before the turn of the century.

Henry Ford's ideas were as brilliant from the standpoint of marketing as they were from the standpoint of mechanics. Ford perceived the need to transform the automobile from a luxury to a necessity by making cars cheap and making them simple to operate. His was a car everyone could afford. In its heydey, the flivver sold for about $400. Ford's concept succeeded beyond his wildest dreams, and the Tin Lizzie transformed the face of America. Its success enabled Ford to retire at an early age, whereupon he took up sailing to avoid the traffic jams he had created.

DOLPHINS ARE THE WORLD'S most uneasy sleepers. They nap only a few hours at a stretch—with one eye open at all times!

THE WORD *ye* in such expressions as "Ye Olde Shoppe" is pronounced like the word *the*. The letter *y* in Anglo-Saxon indicated the same *th* sound apparent in the current spelling.

AROUND 1850, A CHAP by the name of Loy, who lived in London, made a most unusual pair of skates. The springs across the instep and across the heel secured the skate to the foot without using screws. The skate was made of satinwood, and enriched by plates of gilded metalwork. A swan's neck was a graceful and appropriate ornament.

THE RINCONADA RACETRACK in Venezuela—called the most luxurious track in the world—has a swimming pool for horses.

A LEAPING FLEA accelerates from a standstill to a speed of three feet per second in less than two-thousandths of a second, subjecting the insect to a gravitational force of 150G. This is roughly equivalent to driving a car into a brick wall at 200 m.p.h.

The Puniest Pisces

The smallest fish in the world is the *Pandaka pygmea*, found in certain creeks in the Philippines. It reaches an average width of six-sixteenths of an inch, and an average length of seven-sixteenths of an inch. It is no bigger than an ant, and it is probably the tiniest creature with a backbone that has ever been isolated. The slender body of this fish is virtually transparent and the only clearly visible features are its comparatively large eyes.

AN ALTIMETER, AS YOU might have guessed, measures altitude. Used primarily in airplanes and balloons, the device is generally a type of barometer. But the altimeter differs from the barometer in that it can indicate the distance that one is above the surface of the ground.

Some altimeters, such as an airplane's terrain-clearance indicator, utilize radio waves. The altimeter measures the time taken for a wave to be sent from the plane to the ground and back, converts this time into feet, and thus indicates the distance between the plane and the ground.

Fishy Business

Try as you might, you won't find the word *sardine* on any list of fish species, for strictly speaking there is no such thing as a sardine. What we eat as sardines are actually any of a number of small, thin-boned fish, usually herring or pilchards, that are suitable for packing in oil. Conceivably, a can of sardines may contain fish of a number of different species.

AT NOON, ON A spring day in Paris in 1910, a truck broke down in the center of the Place de l'Opera. The driver got out, went underneath his vehicle, and emerged a half hour later, evidently having made the repair. After apologizing to the police for the traffic snarl he had caused, the man drove away. That night he collected several thousand English pounds from friends whom he had bet that he could lie on his back for 30 minutes at the busiest hour in the busiest traffic center in Paris. The man's name was Horace De Vere Cole, England's greatest practical joker of the day.

HARRODS, A LARGE department store in London, is blessed with three private wells on its Knightsbridge property.

A Seedy Shave

In Panama, a Guaymi Indian need never buy a razor. When he wants a shave, he just wanders to the edge of a grassy field and pulls one of the thick, high stalks. He removes one of the oatlike seeds that grow in bunches on each stalk. On the sides of each of these seeds are two slender blades that are as sharp as glass.

Holding the seed firmly by its tough filaments, the Guaymi draws it across his face, and off go his whiskers. He couldn't get a cleaner shave in a barber shop.

IN 1864, IN RESPONSE to an outcry against trains, the British government passed a law which limited steam-driven vehicles to a speed of 4 m.p.h. in the country and 2 m.p.h. in the city.

THE LEFT BANK of a river is the bank to the left of a person looking *downstream*, and has nothing at all to do with the right-left relationship of the two banks on a map. Thus, St. Louis is on the right bank of the Mississippi, and Manhattan Island forms part of the left bank of the Hudson.

The Way of All Whiskers

It was, of course, the hippies who started the current style of long hair, beard, whiskers, and sideburns—more properly called burnsides, after the Confederate general who sported this particular brand of hirsute adornment. The hippies, and their forerunners, the beats, who rebelled against the foppery of fancy duds and the time-wastefulness of trimming away the indicia of manliness, can be said to have become a social force just around the time Jack Kerouac wrote *On the Road* in 1957. The hippy paean struck its high note with the presentation of "Hair," which celebrated the most visible aspect of hippiness.

Yet it is now being bruited about that the beard has reached the heydey of its current vogue, and may well be on the way out—or off, as the case may be. Indeed, love for the beard has been very fickle. During the first part of this century—between 1910 and 1960—facial foliage in the United States was indeed a rarity.

AN APOLLO SPACECRAFT develops more power on lift-off than all the automobiles in England put together.

IF YOU WERE to place one grain of rice on the first square of a chessboard, then two grains on the second square, four on the third, eight on the fouth, and so on, you would never have enough rice to complete the task. To fill the last square you would need 2^{63} grains of rice— enough rice to bury the state of New York and all its inhabitants.

Any Requests?

An ingenious Californian by the name of Dr. Cecil Nixon constructed a robot in 1940 with uncommon abilities. The doctor, who named his creation Isis, fashioned the instrument in the form of the ancient Egyptian goddess. Isis rested on a couch with a zither on her lap.

The instrument could play any of about 3,000 tunes if asked to do so by anyone within a 12-foot radius. This came about because Isis was constructed so that voice vibrations touched off her complicated mechanism. Isis' right hand picked out the melody on the zither, while her left hand performed the accompaniment.

The machinery inside of Isis included 1,187 wheels and 370 electromagnets. There were numerous other parts. As a crowning touch, Dr. Nixon made Isis react to a warm temperature. When she got hot, she would remove the veil from her face all by herself.

It is not known what has happened to Isis in the 30-odd years since she was built. Apparently, she is not on exhibition anymore.

IF UPON THEIR ARRIVAL in Bethlehem the Three Wise Men had invested one dollar at four percent interest, their account would now be worth a quantity of gold 100,000 times the size of the earth!

HERE'S ONE FOR Western fans: a 10-gallon hat actually holds 3/4 of a gallon.

TO ESCAPE ITS many enemies, a flying fish shoots out of the water and glides as far as 500 feet on its greatly enlarged fins. Some of the most powerful of flying fish can even jump over the deck of a small ship.

AT ANY GIVEN MOMENT there are more than 2,000 thunderstorms brewing in the earth's atmosphere.

THE SUN GIVES the sea its blue color. Actually, pure sea water is colorless. The surface water absorbs all but the blue rays of the sun. But the sea reflects back the blue rays to make the ocean traveler think the water itself is blue.

THERE ARE 156 languages in the world each of which is spoken by at least one million people.

Cat on Cue

David Belasco's 1879 play *Hearts of Oak* began with a cat walking out from under an armchair and stretching before a log fire. Theatre-goers were puzzled as to how the animal could be taught such perfect timing. Months later, Belasco revealed that before curtain time each night, the cat was squeezed into a box hidden under the chair and, as the curtain rose, released from its temporary prison by means of an offstage cord. The cat then naturally crawled out and stretched its cramped muscles.

A Journey to Dreamland

Dreams are similar to hallucinations in that they are not usually caused by sense impressions. To be sure, a toothache or indigestion may affect the form of the dream, but it will not determine the content of the dream. While the duration of a dream is a matter of dispute among scientists, many believe that even the most image-crowded dream lasts but a few seconds. All dreams occur in living color.

What gives the dream its restorative power? Little is known for certain about the dream world, but Freud believed that dreams provide a safety valve for suppressed desires, and that dreams actually protect sleep by draining off the emotional turmoil that would otherwise cause a person to wake up.

So many of us have so much trouble getting to sleep in the first place that nearly half a billion dollars are spent annually in the United States on sleeping pills.

THE GRAND CANAL in China, which connects the Yellow and the Yangtze Rivers, is twenty times as long as the Panama Canal—yet the Chinese waterway was built without modern equipment 1,300 years ago!

THE MOST COSTLY punctuation error of all time was committed in November, 1962, when the omission of a hyphen from a set of directions transmitted to a U.S. Venus space probe rocket resulted in the rocket's destruction.

AN UNCONFIRMED REPORT to the United States Weather Bureau states that on July 6, 1949, a freak heat wave on the central coast of Portugal resulted in a temperature of 158 degrees, which lasted for two minutes.

Radio—Alive and Well

Reports of the death of radio are, like those about Mark Twain, greatly exaggerated. More radios were sold in the U.S. in 1971—18,579,000—than in any previous year. And this was more than twice the number of radios sold in 1937, in the "golden age of radio." Today, there are approximately 630 million radios being listened to all over the world. About 354 million of these are in the United States and its possessions—about one and a half sets for every man, woman, and child.

The history of radio begins before Marconi, with the studies of electromagnetic waves conducted by Heinrich Hertz and James Clark Maxwell. But it was Guglielmo Marconi who, in 1895, gave the first demonstration of radio-telegraphy. During the following year, he secured a patent for his system of communication; and in 1901, he accomplished the first transatlantic transmission.

THE WORLD'S FASTEST ANIMAL is the cheetah. It has been timed at 70 miles per hour, but many believe that it can do even better over a short haul. Sometimes called the hunting leopard, the cheetah has long been used in India to track down the black buck, the Indian antelope, and other fast game.

THE PRODUCERS OF THE 1947 spectacular *Caesar and Cleopatra* were perfectionists indeed. For a moonlight scene beside the Sphinx, a set was designed which showed hundreds of stars in the sky in the exact position they occupied over the Egyptian desert in the year 45 B.C.

THE TRUNK OF an elephant can hold six quarts of water— enough to wash down the biggest snootful of peanuts.

High Fashion

During the 17th century, high heeled shoes became fashionable in Venice. Eventually the heels became so high that women could not walk in them, and servants were hired so that the ladies could lean on them while getting in and out of a gondola.

THE ONLY GESTURE man does not share with any other animal is the smile.

THE LONGEST OF ALL WORMS is the *Lineus longissimus,* or "living fishing line worm." In 1964, a specimen washed ashore at St. Andrews, Scotland, after a storm. It measured more than 180 feet in length.

DESPITE THE FACT that the jew's harp has to be held between the teeth and its tone modulated by movements of the mouth, Charles Eulenstein of Germany could play 16 in different keys at one time. The 19th-century virtuoso accomplished this feat by fastening the instruments to a stand on a level with his lips.

WHEN CERTAIN AFRICAN natives need sutures for first aid, they just dig up a few driver ants and use the insects' huge jaws to clamp together the edges of their wounds.

THE LONGEST STREET in the world that runs through the same city is Figueroa Street, in Los Angeles, which runs north and south through the city for a distance of 30 miles.

DOMESTICATED HORSES have been bred for centuries in almost every country in the world, but of the 38 best-known breeds now in existence, 16 were created in Great Britain. Only four breeds are distinctly American: the Morgan, the Mustang, the American Saddle Horse, and the Hambletonian.

Locomotive Lore
If railroad trains could be run as efficiently as their model counterparts, rail travel would be significantly improved. The record run by a toy train was achieved at Nuremberg, Germany, in 1971, by a Fleischmann "Black Elephant" HO gauge engine. The tiny workhorse pulled a 62-axle train 1,053 miles over its miniature track without stopping. At scale, this was equivalent to a run of 11,600 miles—more than two round-trips between New York and Los Angeles—at a speed of 123.9 m.p.h. Try to find a train that can match that record!

A TORNADO THAT STRUCK St. Louis in 1927 caused $26 million worth of damage in five minutes.

A Colorful Tune

Green with Envy, Purple with Passion, White with Anger, Scarlet with Fever, What Were You Doing in Her Arms Last Night Blues is the title—the longest known title to date—of a tune written by Phillip Springer and Nita Jones in 1961.

IF YOU TRIED to pay the month's rent or your bus fare with cigarettes, people would laugh at you. But in pre-Revolutionary America, tobacco was acceptable legal tender in several Southern colonies. Virginia even enacted a law that taxes should be payed in tobacco.

OF THE 250 known alphabets in the history of language, 50 are still alive today. Half of these are in India.

WHEN ACTIVE, the Paricutin volcano in central Mexico could spew 4 million pounds of rock and lava into the air in one minute.

EVEN WHEN YOU'RE standing still, you're actually traveling at incredibly high speeds. The earth is revolving at the speed of 1,000 miles per hour, and orbiting the sun at the speed of 66,700 miles per hour.

ON OCTOBER 8, 1929, a milestone in modern transportation was reached when a newsreel and two cartoons were shown on a Transcontinental Air Transport plane.

A Timely Tale
In the famous cathedral of Notre Dame de Dijon in France, there is the oldest gong clock in the world. Given to the town of Dijon in 1383 by Philip the Hardy, this clock has been keeping abreast of the time ever since. Constructed by Jacques Marc, the clock contains two large bronze figures which have struck the hour every hour for the last 590 years. An ambitious mathematician computed that by January 1, 1950, these bronze figures had struck the clock 32,284,980 times.

AMONG HIS MANY claims to fame, Benjamin Franklin can list the honor of being the first spelling reform advocate in the United States. In 1768, Franklin proposed a scheme to reform English spelling with a new alphabet. He advocated dropping the letters *c*, *j*, *q*, *w*, *x*, and *y*, and substituting six new characters so that every sound in the language could be expressed with one letter.

THROUGH THE CENTURIES, man has made a great to-do about his hair. Some of the ancients went to great extremes in caring for their beards. The Lords of Nineveh oiled and curled their beards. The Kings of Persia plaited their hirsutulous draperies with golden thread. Early French kings daintily tied their whiskers with silken ribbons. Even today, the Sikhs of India dye their beards, for it is only a flaming red patch that will establish a Sikh as a man among men.

BETWEEN DAWN AND DUSK an acre of peas can increase in weight by 50 percent, owing to the vegetable's high rate of absorption.

PEOPLE BEGIN TO shrink after the age of thirty.

Modern Monickers

If you're thumbing through an old book and come across a reference to a city or nation that you've never heard of, the chances are good that you've merely stumbled onto the old name for a well-known place. Among the more recent place-name changes are:

Old	New
Ceylon	Sri Lanka
Siam	Thailand
Mesopotamia	Iraq
Persia	Iran
Ciudad Trujillo	Santo Domingo
Christiania	Oslo
Stalingrad	Volgograd
St. Petersburg	Leningrad
Gold Coast	Ghana
Belgian Congo	Zaire
Tanganyika	Tanzania
Constantinople	Istanbul
Peiping	Peking
East Pakistan	Bangladesh
Northern Rhodesia	Zambia
Danzig	Gdansk
Batavia	Djakarta

A MICROPHONE PLACED a few inches away from a toci-toci beetle will not detect the insect's gentle rapping on a stone. Yet a female toci-toci beetle can pick up the vibrations of these mating signals from up to five miles away.

IN A ROAD-SAFETY CAMPAIGN, English police in Sussex asked girl pedestrians to wear miniskirts because bare legs stand out more clearly at night than long dresses or slacks.

IF IN 1600, you happened to be walking along a Dutch canal, you might have been surprised to see a two-masted ship bearing down on you. Not in the canal—on the road. There was one such ship that was said to have reached a speed of 20 mph while carrying 28 fear-stricken passengers. In his notebooks, Leonardo da Vinci had envisioned some sort of self-propelled vehicle; and some Dutchman, quite naturally, had modeled such a vehicle after a sailing vessel.

A MOTHER COD can lay as many as five million eggs at a single spawning—of which only a half dozen usually survive. If all cod eggs produced live fish, there would be no room left in the ocean for water.

DURING THE 21-YEAR-PLUS London run of the Agatha Christie play *The Mousetrap,* wardrobe mistress Maisie Wilmer-Brown ironed her way through 36 miles of shirts.

THE NEST OF the bald eagle provides a life-long home for its majestic occupant, and through continual renovation an aerie can weigh over a ton. One eagle's nest at Vermillon, Ohio, measured 12 feet deep and weighed two tons. Try that one in your back-yard aviary!

Smoking Out the Smokers
These days, pipes, cigars, and cigarillos are taking an increasing share of the tobacco sales, while the popularity of non-filter cigarettes has declined precipitously in recent years. Yet the Surgeon General's report on the hazards of smoking has hardly meant the last gasp for filtered cigarettes. More filtered cigarettes are now sold each year than the year before. Demon nicotine seems to have secured a niche in the American way of life.

And, by the way, it was Europe—not the United States—that developed the filter cigarette. America only lays claim to the invention of the smoker's cough.

BRANDY IS OBTAINED from wine or the fermented mash of fruit. It is made from grapes, or cherries, or apples, or plums, or apricots, or peaches, or blackberries.

THE NATION WITH the highest beer consumption is Belgium. The average Belgian enjoys 30.6 gallons of the frothy nectar each year. In the Northern Territory of Australia, however, beer consumption has been unofficially estimated to be close to 52 gallons per person each year.

THE SEARS, ROEBUCK COMPANY is the largest retailing company in the United States. In 1973, Sears totaled over $10 billion in sales—almost twice as much as its nearest competitor for top honors, the Atlantic and Pacific Tea Company (A & P).

I'll Take Mine Black, Please

Surprisingly enough, coffee, which accounts for a staggering $2 billion a year in international trade, didn't reach Brazil until a mere 250 years ago. The coffee tree, indigenous only to Arabia and Ethiopia, was supposedly discovered by goats. They ate the wild-growing berries and began to cavort in the fields, convincing their goatherd to join them in a cup.

The Arabs were cultivating the plant as early as 600 A.D., and used the berries as medicine. It wasn't until the 13th century that it was discovered how to brew coffee into a beverage. For the next 400 years, the Arabs jealously guarded the coffee trade, exercising a monopoly by forbidding the export of fertile seeds on pain of death.

But about 1700, Dutch traders managed to smuggle out some plants, sending the embezzled botanica to the island of Java, where the growth became so prolific, the island's name became synonymous with the brew.

As MANY AS 1,652 languages and dialects are spoken by India's 600 million people. Hindi, the official language, is spoken by only 35 percent of the population.

THE MOST COMMON SURNAME in the United States is Smith. Close to 2.5 million Smiths reside here, half a million more than those with the second most common name, Johnson.

THE LARGEST CRABS in the world—which live off the coast of Japan—stand three feet high and often weigh as much as 30 pounds.

IN 18TH-CENTURY AMERICA, portraitists journeyed from town to town with an assortment of paintings of men and women, complete in every feature except the faces. A person wishing to sit for his portrait simply had to select the body he liked best, and let the artist fill in the missing face and hair.

Who Put the "Green" in Greenland?

There is very little green in Greenland, for the island is covered with ice and snow for most of the year. According to legend, the misnomer was given to the land by the Scandinavian explorer Eric the Red in an attempt to induce followers to settle on the barren island.

SNOW IS NOT frozen rain. Snowflakes change directly from water vapor into snow, without going through an intermediary stage as rain.

AN OSTRICH CANNOT FLY, but the 400-pound bird can outrun many racehorses.

Jealous Genius

Michelangelo—the great Renaissance painter, sculptor, architect, and poet—signed only one of his many works: the *Pietà* in St. Peter's. The artist chiseled his name and birthplace on the figure of Mary after hearing a group of sightseers erroneously attribute the work to another sculptor.

THE FIRST BOARDWALK erected in the United States was located in Atlantic City, New Jersey. The eight-foot wide walkway was completed in 1870 and rested directly on top of the sand.

IN 1970, a limbo dancer from the West Indies, Theresa Marquis, limboed her way under a bar only six and one half inches above the ground. Try to match that record.

Model Tea

In 2737 B.C., says Chinese legend, leaves from a wild tea bush fell by chance into the Emperor Shen Nung's boiling drinking water. "What a delightful flavor!" said the wise Emperor, drinking the world's first cup of tea.

The Chinese poet, Lu-Yu, published the first book about tea in 780 A.D. Wait till the water boils, he tells us, and when the bubbles resemble crystal beads rolling in a fountain, it is time to pour the water over the tea leaves.

THE FASTEST SPEED at which a giant tortoise can crawl is about 5 yards a minute. A rabbit can cover the same distance in less than a half-second.

OF THE MORE THAN 500 elephants that have been exhibited in the United States, only six are known to have been conceived and born here.

ONLY EIGHT BREEDS of purebred dog originated in the United States: the American foxhound, American water spaniel, Boston terrier, Chesapeake Bay retriever, Coonhound, Amertoy, Spitz, and Staffordshire terrier. The British Isles holds the pedigreed pouch title—of the world's 163 recognized breeds, 47 originated there.

THE FIRST SUCCESSFUL electric elevator was installed in the Demarest Building in New York City, in 1889.

A Shaggy Dog Story

Between 1892 and 1902, a small mongrel named Tim— with a metal collection box attached to his collar—met all incoming trains in London's Paddington Station to beg for coins for the widows' and orphans' fund of a British railroad. When the animal died, his body was placed in a glass case in the station, with a slot for coins so that the dog could continue his work.

THE GUARDS AT THE JAIL in Alamos, Mexico, may well be the most vigilant in the world. Regulations at Alamos provide that a guard must serve out the sentence of any prisoner who escapes while he is on duty.

THE TERM *drawing room* has nothing to do with sketching. The word *drawing* is actually a shortening of *withdrawing*—for this was the room to which guests "withdrew."

Jeweled Jahangir

Of the many collectors of glittering jewels down through the ages, Emperor Jahangir, the noble ruler of India who died in 1627, is the most noted who ever lived. It is reported that he owned a total of 2,235,600 carats of pearls, 931,500 carats of emeralds, 376,600 carats of rubies, 279,450 carats of diamonds, and 186,300 carats of jade.

For his time, Jahangir was an enlightened monarch. During his reign, architectural masterpieces rose throughout India.

One of the emperor's hobbies was fishing, but Jahangir never killed a fish he caught. Instead, he would place a string of pearls through the fish's gills and throw it back into the water.

If nothing else, the man was extremely vain, for his name itself, Jahangir, means "Conqueror of the World." In addition, he had other glorious titles such as "Possessor of the Planets," "Mirror of the Glories of God," and "King of Increasing Fortune."

ABOUT 525 SONGS and instrumental pieces were written about Abraham Lincoln, the largest number ever produced in honor of a secular individual. Approximately 450 of these compositions were published between his campaign in 1860 and his assassination in 1865. They comprise campaign and nomination selections, presidential hymns, emancipation songs, and minstrel and comic pieces. The other 75 consist of some 50 funeral marches and 25 memorial pieces.

AT FULL MATURITY, Claude Seurat—the skinniest man who ever lived—had a back-to-chest thickness of only three inches.

AN ANGRY LLAMA will spit in his antagonist's face.

Scraping Bottom

The brilliant pink flamingo goes to the unappetizing bottoms of lakes and bogs for its meals. Standing in fairly shallow water, it plunges its head and long neck straight down into the mud so that it seems to be standing on its head.

With the upper part of its beak, the flamingo scoops up the mud. Then it strains the mud through its specially built, immovable lower beak. What's left—small mollusks and other little creatures—it eats.

THE FLAG OF Denmark is the oldest unchanged national flag in existence, dating back to the 13th century.

IN THE MIDDLE OF the 14th century, in Spain, there arose a vogue of wearing false beards. In the morning, a grandee dandy would drape his chin in a crimson beard; in the evening, he serenaded his señorita in an adjustable, long, black hanging. Soon the country resembled a huge masquerade party. No one knew who was who. Creditors could not catch up with debtors. The police arrested the innocent while villains hid behind hair. Wives were conjugal with the wrong husbands, whereupon the price of horsehair skyrocketed. King Peter of Aragon had to end the farce by forbidding the wearing of false beards.

THE WORLD'S TINIEST plant seeds are those of the *Epiphytic* orchid. They come 35,000,000 to the ounce!

THE FLEA IS the world's champion high jumper. This mighty mite can accomplish a leap 80 times its own height and 150 times its length. If a man could do the same, he would be capable of leaping over a building 50 stories high and three football fields long.

THE UNITED STATES produces more than twice as many cars each year as babies.

WHAT'RE THE ODDS against a coin coming up heads fifty times in a row? Well, according to one calculation, a million men would each have to toss a coin ten times every minute for 40 hours a week in order to achieve an occurence of 50 straight heads just once in nine centuries.

Protective Custody

A hornbill must find just the right size hole in a tree for a nest. The female slips inside and there lays her eggs.

The male seals off the entrance with mud, leaving only a narrow slit. Inside, the female is both protected and imprisoned while incubating her eggs. She gets food from her mate by sticking her bill out of the slit. When the young are full grown, the seal is broken, and the young leave the home with their mother.

TWELVE ARCHITECTS SPENT most of their lives working on the construction of St. Peter's Church, in Rome. Most of them never lived to see the church completed.

The Facts on Fossils

A fossil can be either the actual remains of a plant or an animal, or the imprint of a plant or animal, preserved from prehistoric times by nature. Quick burial in material that excludes bacteria and oxygen prevents decay and permits whole preservation. Preservation for aeons creates fossils. The scientific study of fossils is called paleontology.

Insects that lived millions of years ago are often found in amber. This hard substance was originally a sticky resin which enveloped the insect. Through the years, the fragile tissues of the insect dried, until all that remained was the mold, sometimes so precise scientists can conduct microscopic studies of its structure.

Fossilization is often the result of petrification. Mineral material from underground streams may be deposited in the interstices of bones, shells, or plants, and render the subject more stonelike, thus protecting it from the ravages of time. Over the millennia, the original live material may be replaced entirely by minerals, so that the original structure and appearance are maintained, as in petrified wood. Petrified logs from the Triassic period may be seen in the Petrified Forest of Arizona.

DON'T EVER ACCUSE the chicken of being behind the times. In the 1930's, the average American hen laid 121 eggs a year. Today, a hen donates about 217 eggs to the breakfast tables of America.

"A" IS THE FIRST letter of every alphabet except the old German, in which it is the fourth, and the Ethiopian, in which it is the 13th.

Shake, Rattle, and Roll

There's a certain art in even such a seemingly simple activity as shaking fruit from a tree. In general, a hard, slow shake is preferable to a quick, short motion. But for each fruit there's a specific frequency that's best. Plums, for example, will fall about three times as freely if the plum tree is shaken 400 times a minute, two inches per shake, than they would at 1,100 times a minute, one inch per shake. Cherries respond most favorably to 1,200 short shakes per minute, while apple trees are most generous when shaken 400 times per minute.

THE MOSCOW TO PEKING run on the Trans-Siberian Railroad is the longest rail journey that can be made without changing trains.

THE WHYOS, A BROOKLYN gang of mobsters who preceded the Five Points gang, issued a printed list for potential clients: "Punching, $2; both eyes blacked, $4; nose and jaw broken, $10; jacked out (stunned with a blackjack), $15; ear chewed off, $15; leg or arm broken, $19; shot in leg, $25; stabbed, $25; doing the big job, $100."

All in a Day's Work

Despite appearances, bees do not wander aimlessly from flower to flower in search of nectar. Many flowers produce nectar at only certain times of the day, and bees follow a timetable which brings them to the right flower at just the right time. A bee's busy day may begin with a dandelion at nine in the morning, continue with a blue cornflower at eleven o'clock, then a red clover at one o'clock, and a viper at about three—for those are the hours at which each of these flowers is most generous with its nectar.

FUNERAL DIRECTORS IN California are offering a new economy deal—for only $25 your ashes will be scattered over the Pacific Ocean from a light aircraft. A certificate will be issued guaranteeing the time at which your ashes were "committed to the elements of the eternal seven seas."

A SCIENTIST AT the University of Arizona has developed a heat-sensitive instrument for taking temperature readings from distant planets. This device is so sensitive that it could detect a lit match across the breadth of the Pacific Ocean.

A Ticklish Situation

One of the oldest—and strangest—methods of fishing is practiced by the Maoris of New Zealand. The Maori fishermen wade out into the clear stream or lake, moving very quietly so as not to create ripples. Here fish swim in and out of clumps of rock or coral, sometimes stopping for a quick nap. Half of the fish may be hidden by the rock, but the rest of the fish juts out into view.

Wading up behind the fish, the silent Maori will reach down and tickle the fish's sides. In trying to wriggle away, the fish backs out of his hiding place and lands right in the fisherman's hands. The stealthy tickler must be very adept to hold onto his slippery supper.

THE FASTEST DOG in the world is either the saluki or the greyhound, depending on whom you talk to. The greyhound has been clocked at 41.7 miles per hour.

THE DAY WAS August 19, 1962. Longview, Texas was agog. Homero Blancas, a 24-year-old graduate of the University of Houston, had just completed the first round of the Premier Invitational Tournament in 55 strokes! His card of 27 for the front nine and 28 for the back was the lowest round of golf ever played on a course measuring more than 5,000 yards.

IN MEDIEVAL FRANCE, King Philip Augustus decreed that the points on his subjects' shoes should be between six and twelve inches, depending upon their station—the longer the point, the higher the rank.

AN INN IN Soleure, Switzerland, called the *Krone*, still possesses a bill for 1,417 Swiss francs charged to Napoleon's troops for an opulent meal and other amenities in 1797. Although a lavish feast had been prepared for Napoleon, the General merely drank a glass of water and moved on.

IN 1793, A GIRL in Tourcoing, France, was born with only one eye—in the center of her forehead! Otherwise normal, the girl lived to the age of 15.

A Long Talk

At 12:30 p.m. on June 12, 1935, Senator Huey Long of Louisiana began a filibuster in the Senate. When Long finally dropped into his seat from physical exhaustion at 4 a.m. the following day, he had been speaking continually for 15½ hours—the longest speech on record. The speech was 150,000 words long and included such irrelevancies as cooking recipes and humorless anecdotes. Long's marathon monologue filled 100 pages in the *Congressional Record*, and cost the Government $5,000 to print.

SHAMPOO, WHICH TO US means to wash your hair, comes from the Hindu word *shampu*, which means to press. A good shampoo is one where you press your fingers hard against your scalp, so our word still indicates part of the original Hindu meaning.

Canine Comparisons

Of the many thousands of dogs registered by the American Kennel Club, in 1970 there were only four breeds in which there were less than five dogs registered. It appears that throughout the entire United States there were only four Sussex Spaniels on record, only three Belgian Malinois, only two Field Spaniels, and only two English Foxhounds.

Compare these, for example, with 61,042 Dachshunds, or with 13,180 Great Danes, or even with 769 Irish Wolfhounds.

CHOCOLATE, THE BANE of adolescent complexions and bulgy midriffs, is a preparation made from the seeds of the cacao tree. The Aztecs favored a chocolate beverage which they introduced to the Spanish explorers in the 16th century. This beverage found its way to Europe, where it soon became all the rage. Many chocolate shops became centers of political discussion, such as the famous *Cocoa Tree* in London.

SINCE THE VIOLIN was introduced in the 1600's, several devices have been invented for playing the instrument automatically. But the only one to vibrate the strings with a bow was the *violonista,* which could be found in penny arcades in the early 1920's. The machine was about three feet long, two feet high, and two feet wide. It was electrically operated and controlled by air flowing through the perforations of a music roll.

Two women—a Russian and an Austrian—have given
birth to 69 children. Neither woman ever gave birth to
less than two children in one confinement.

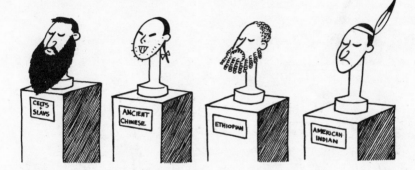

THE GROWTH OF BEARDS varies considerably among the
peoples of the earth. The Celts and Slavs have the most
luxurious appendages; the Chinese, but a few hairlets;
the Ethiopians, a curly beard; and the American
Indians, hardly any tuft at all.

IN THE 16TH CENTURY, the Spaniards introduced the
musket, a firearm which enabled a marksman to hit a
target 400 yards away. The intricate reloading
procedure of the musket necessitated the additional
defense of a pike. This drawback of the musket led to
the invention of the bayonet. Rifles were introduced in
the 18th century; and by the 19th century, they became
the standard firearm of all infantry.

THE NATION WITH the highest reported murder rate is Luxembourg, with 14.4 murders per 100,000 population. The lowest reported rate is that of Norway, 0.1 per 100,000. The U.S. rate is 8.5.

Where There's Smoke . . .

No one is quite certain that Rodrigo de Jerez of Spain was the first European to smoke tobacco, but he is more often credited with that distinction than anyone else. As the story has it, he learned to smoke from the natives of the West Indies where he landed with Columbus in 1492. When he returned to Spain, he brought a bit of the plant with him, and greatly astonished the populace by his newly acquired habit. His wife denounced him to the Inquisition as a man who "swallows fire, exhales smoke, and is surely possessed by the devil."

IN 1195, THE Sultan of Marrakesh, Morocco, ordered that 960 sacks of musk be added to the mortar for a minaret he was building to commemorate a military victory. That minaret still stands, and the fragrance of the musk can be perceived today.

A Fish Story

The largest fish ever caught by any method was a 17-foot-long, 4,500-pound white shark, harpooned by Frank Mundus off Montauk Point, Long Island, New York in 1964.

The largest fish ever caught by rod and reel was a white shark measuring 16 feet 10 inches long and weighing 2,664 pounds. It was brought in by Alf Dean at Denial Bay, near Ceduna, South Australia, on April 21, 1959.

A CURLEW CAN FLY non-stop for more than 2,000 miles. Most of the bird's flight is over water, so the curlew doesn't have much of a choice about taking a breather. He can't swim!

THE LONGEST MAN-MADE OBJECT in the world is an oil pipeline which stretches 1,775 miles between Alberta and Ontario, Canada. But an oil pipeline being constructed in the Soviet Union will be 2,860 miles long.

IF YOU THINK Adelle Davis brewed up a storm over nutrition, you should have been around when Sylvester Graham, the father of the graham cracker, was stirring up the country with his lectures and books in the 1830's-1840's. He antagonized thousands by opposing such standard commodities as tea, coffee, tobacco, liquor, meat, corsets, and featherbeds. He also persuaded thousands to follow his diet, which included bread made of coarse flour, since known as Graham flour. The number of Grahamites became so great that, to accommodate them, scores of Graham boarding houses were established, and restaurants set apart special Graham tables.

THE LARGEST LITTER ever thrown was 23, by a fox-hound called Lena, on February 11, 1945.

Speed Demon—19th-Century Style

Chicagoans were out in force on Thanksgiving Day, 1895. They came to see a new-fangled contraption called an automobile. A few of the gasoline-powered horseless carriages were going to race.

The route lay from the heart of Chicago to a nearby suburb and back. The road measured exactly 54.36 miles. The winner would have to cover that terrific distance without breaking down.

J. Frank Duryea busted the tape seven hours and 17 minutes after the start of the race. He had covered the distance at an average speed of 7.5 miles an hour! The crowd went wild!

A FLYING HONEYBEE beats its wings 250 times a second; the housefly, 190 times a second.

Metric Measure

The two systems of measurement now in use are the Metric and the English system. Oddly enough, the English have recently converted to the metric system.

The meter is defined in terms of lightwaves. According to this definition, one meter is equivalent to 1,533,164.12 wave lengths of the red light emitted by cadmium.

YOU MOST LIKELY have never noticed, but characters in animated cartoons are usually drawn with only three fingers and a thumb to save time and labor.

ESKIMO BOYS OF three and four years old may be seen smoking pipes! Little girls are not allowed the privilege. A father is very proud when his son picks up the knack, for smoking is considered a sign of manliness.

PIANOFORTE COMES FROM two Italian words: *piano* which means soft, and *forte* which means loud. So pianoforte actually means "soft-loud." The piano, which is what most of us call a pianoforte, was the first keyboard instrument ever invented which could play both soft and loud.

Solace for Southpaws

There are no records of the exact beginning of discrimination against lefthanders, but as far back as Rome, right was right; which means to say that *dextra,* from which comes our word *dextrous* or *handy,* means right in Latin. But how did the Romans designate the other side? Anything that was left was *sinistra* (sinister). Even the Old English, who gave us the word *left,* used it to mean *weak.* Now is that fair?

Fighting a ratio of five righthanders for every lefthander, lefthanders have risen to the challenge. Da Vinci worked with his left hand. A study of Einstein's brainwaves indicated that his right hemisphere—the side responsible for the responses on the left side of the body—was more highly developed than his left.

The Miracle, one of the most spectacular dramas ever presented in the United States, required a cast of 700 and a theatre redesigned to resemble a Gothic Cathedral. When the play went on the road, a train of 204 cars was needed to transport the actors and equipment.

THE RAREST AND most valuable button in the world is the "Morse" or "Cope" button, a magnificent work of art fashioned by Benvenuto Cellini in 1530 for Pope Clement VI. A large, round, and flat button measuring six inches in diameter, it is made of gold and encrusted with gems. Over the beautiful diamond at the center is an image of God the Father. According to his *Autobiography*, Cellini worked 18 months on this one button and employed a staff of 10 artisans to help him.

THE NATIONS OF Iceland, Costa Rica, and Liechtenstein have no armed forces.

FOR ECONOMY AND EASE, you can't beat the food-gathering methods of the Cistercian Monastery in Alcobaca, Portugal. Whenever its cooks want fresh fish, all they do is lower their nets into a branch of the Alcoa River which flows through the heart of their huge kitchen.

THE MOST FAMOUS of all golf courses and clubs is the Royal and Ancient of St. Andrews. Founded in 1774, its basic rules were soon accepted throughout the world. After 1888, the game gained in popularity in the United States, the year when the St. Andrews Golf Club of Westchester County, New York, was founded.

THE CHEMICAL THAT gives the skunk his malodorous reputation is called *ethanethiol*, a substance so pungent that less than one ten-trillionth (.000,000,000,000,1) of an ounce can be detected by the human nose.

THE FIRST ADVERTISED radio broadcast was transmitted from Brant Rock, Massachusetts, on Christmas Eve of 1906 by Professor Reginald Aubrey Fessenden. But the first radio station with a regular broadcasting schedule—KDKA of Pittsburgh, Pennsylvania—did not come on the scene until 1920. Today, there are more than 4,370 A.M. stations and 2,350 F.M. stations broadcasting in the U.S.

Weather or Not

The first thermometers, devised independently by Galileo and Sanctorius at the turn of the 17th century, consisted essentially of a bulb atop a stem which descended into a liquid. Heating or cooling the bulb affected the height of the column of liquid in the tube, which was marked by a scale.

About a hundred years later, in 1714, Fahrenheit of Danzig invented the mercury thermometer to measure heat. The thermometer of Reaumur, invented about 15 years later, used alcohol to measure cold. Mercury was not feasible for this thermometer because mercury solidifies at -39°C.

The centigrade thermometer, created by Celsius in 1742, is used primarily in laboratory work. It has the computational advantage of a 100-degree range between the freezing point and the boiling point.

Pandora's Box

There was a time when jewelry boxes were equipped with devices that killed anyone who attempted to open them without knowing the secret. One such case, sold at auction in New York several years ago, stood about 14 inches high by 20 inches wide and 10 inches deep. It had a bottom lock for the box, and a top lock for the protective mechanisms. If the top lock was open when the case was opened, the four doors instantly flew open, a pistol sprang into position behind each door, and all four pistols fired automatically.

A Breech of Fashion

Until the time of the French Revolution, most men wore knee breeches rather than trousers. But in 1789, supporters of the Revolution separated themselves from the royalists by adopting trousers. Accordingly, they were known as the *sans-culottes* ("without breeches").

In token of their sympathy with the French rebels, many ordinary Americans sported trousers between 1790 and 1800. But it was not until a decade or so later that trousers substituted for breeches on formal occasions. The first President who habitually dressed in long trousers was James Madison.

RUM, OBTAINED FROM fermented sugarcane or fermented molasses, is produced primarily in the Caribbean. Different varieties derive from Puerto Rico, Cuba, Jamaica, and Mexico.

WHEN A MANCHURIAN CHILD is ready to learn how to walk, his parents often embroider a cat's head, whiskers and all, on the toes of his shoes. The parents hope that this will make their child as sure-footed as the cat.

WHAT REALLY REVOLUTIONIZED weaponry was the invention of gunpowder, usually attributed to the Chinese firecracker-makers of the 9th century. Gunpowder was introduced into Europe in the 1300's. Field artillery and cannons were first used by the Dutch.

PRINCE WENZEL VON KAUNITZ-RIETBURG, an 18th century Austrian statesman, changed his clothes no less than 30 times daily. This obsession occupied about four hours a day.

THE DOG WHO is reputed to have lived the longest was a black Labrador named "Adjutant," who died on November 30, 1963 at the age of 27 years and three months.

A Bolt from the Blue

The intense heat of lightning is sometimes responsible for odd accidents. One lady's earring was melted by lightning, and another bolt soldered all the links in a one-yard chain. The U.S. National Safety Council's Report for 1943 told of a soldier being welded into his sleeping bag when the zipper was struck by lightning. The startled soldier had to be cut loose.

Talk about automation! In the 1870's, a law firm in the Utah Territory was so deluged with divorce cases that it built a slot machine which sold the necessary papers for $2.50 a set. The papers became legal when signed by both man and woman.

Eureka!

In 214 B.C., a powerful Roman force attacked the city of Syracuse, the home of Archimedes, the great mathematician and astronomer. To hold off the Roman legions, the Greek inventor devised one ingenious weapon after another. Among these weapons was the catapult, which sent a ton of stones flying as far as 600 feet.

But Archimedes' most ingenious contraption was an arrangement of mirrors that directed the concentrated rays of the sun on the Roman ships and set them ablaze.

A CELEBRATED CHINESE ARTIST of the 1920's, Huang Erh-nan, painted beautiful designs on silk cloth—with his tongue as a brush.

MISSOURI AND TENNESSEE both touch on eight other states.

A Stroke of Luck

William Northmore, an inveterate gambler from Okehampton, England, lost his entire fortune of $850,000 on the turn of one card. The townspeople of Okehampton felt so sorry for Northmore that they elected him to Parliament in 1714, and in every election thereafter until his death.

ON SEPTEMBER 13, 1922, the thermometers in Azizia, Libya were about ready to burst. On that day, the temperature in the shade soared to 136 degrees Fahrenheit.

IN 1918, AT Bahia Felix, Chile, rain fell on all but 18 days of the year. And on those 18 it drizzled!

DAVE WHITE'S ROUND at the Winchester Country Club started fine, but he blew up on the fifth hole and took a horrifying 13! Then the Massachusetts pro settled down with a vengeance. He shot 10 straight birdies to salvage a par round of 72.

THE OLD FAITHFUL GEYSER in Yellowstone National Park, Wyoming, spews forth more than 33 million gallons of water each day. That's enough water to provide for the needs of a city of 300,000 people.

A Short Stroll

In 1936, a Norwegian sailor named Mensen Ernst left Constantinople (now Istanbul) on foot and headed east. Crossing mountains, rivers, badlands, and deserts, the 37-year-old Ernst journeyed 2,800 miles to Calcutta—and then turned around and walked back to Constantinople! Ernst made the 5,589-mile round trip in only 59 days.

ONE DAY IN JULY, 1940, John V. Sigmund waded into the Mississippi River at St. Louis and started swimming south. When his friends pulled him out of the drink, a little above Memphis, Sigmund had covered 292 miles. He had been swimming continuously for 89 hours and 42 minutes!

THE LARGEST STRINGED instrument ever constructed for a single player was a pantaleon played by George Noel in England in 1767. Played with wooden mallets like a xylophone, the instrument consisted of 276 gut and metal strings stretched over a horizontal soundboard which was 11 feet long by five feet wide.

ONE OF THE MEN most responsible for the development of the gasoline-powered engine was Carl Benz of Munich, who also supplied one of the first traffic accident statistics. During an exhibition of his 1885 three-wheeled model, he lost control of his car and smashed into a wall. Undaunted, he went on to refine automobile mechanics.

SHAH JEHAN, THE Indian monarch who built the Taj Mahal, planned to build an identical structure on the bank of the Jumma River opposite the Taj. The second structure was to be built of black marble, to contrast with the white Taj, and would have been connected to the Taj by a silver bridge.

The Biggest Bang
The volcanic eruption on Krakatoa in 1883—the loudest and most powerful explosion in history—sent a massive tidal wave halfway around the world. A Dutch warship in the harbor of Batavia (now Djakarta) was washed ashore by the tremendous wave and left stranded a half mile inland and 30 feet above sea level. The wave—which at some points was 120 feet high—traveled 5,450 miles to South Africa in less than 12 hours.

ADOLF KEIFER WON more than 2,000 swimming races. He won his first U.S. championship in 1935, when he was 16 years old. For eight years thereafter the great backstroker was undefeated, and won 24 indoor and outdoor championships.

In 1946, at the time of his retirement from amateur competition, Keifer held every backstroke record in the books. In a brilliant athletic career, Keifer had lost only two races out of more than 2,000!

A Bird's-eye View

The bird on the wing is a symbol of man's aspiration to be more than man, to soar above the natural world. The combination of grace and power epitomized by a bird in flight is both nature's pride and man's joy.

The bird's evolutionary progenitor was the reptile, and several birds—such as the ostrich, the penguin, and the kiwi—remain bound to earth. As the bird moved up the evolutionary scale, it developed many fantastic traits. For example, a bird can focus its eyes more quickly than any other living creature. Its sight is astonishingly keen; so is its sense of hearing; its smell, however, is poor.

CHINESE WOMEN, AS WELL AS the men, enjoy smoking a pipe. Their pipes are extremely delicate and unusually decorated. Cigarettes, on the other hand, which caught on only in the Chinese metropolises before the advent of Mao, are less common in China today than they were 25 years ago.

FOR MANY YEARS, the tobacco habit was bitterly opposed by the English crown and the English church. In his *Counterblast to Tobacco*, King James I described smoking as "a custom loathsome to the eye, hateful to the nose, harmful to the brain, dangerous to the lungs, and in the black stinking fume thereof nearest resembling the horrible Stygian smoke of the pit that is bottomless."

THE FAMOUS MACEDONIAN PHALANX employed a 24-foot-long pike called the sarissa, which permitted a warrior in the sixth fighting rank to extend his arm to the first. This weapon was not subsequently employed by other peoples.

AL CAPONE'S BUSINESS CARD described him as a "second-hand furniture dealer." Capone grossed about $105 million in 1927.

THE TINIEST SNOW CRYSTAL is about 1/500th of an inch in diameter—just a pinpoint. The biggest snowflakes in the world fell in Montana in 1887; they measured 15 inches in diameter and were eight inches thick.

A Close Shave

Peter the Great, Czar of Russia from 1682 until 1725, wanted his countrymen to adopt Western customs and dress. To discourage the growth of beards, which were then unfashionable in Europe, the Czar first levied a tax on all beards, and later decreed that men wearing beards would be shaved by force with a blunt razor, or would have their whiskers removed one by one with a set of pincers. On one occasion, Peter personally cut off the beards of his noblemen.

THE BUDDHIST SAINT, Dengyo Daishi, crossed the sea to Japan in 805 A.D. and planted tea seeds in a temple garden. The plants flourished. In 815 A.D., the Japanese Emperor, Saga, was entertained at a monastery. He liked the tea so well he decreed that the plants be cultivated in the provinces near his capital. By the 10th century, Japan was growing her own tea instead of importing it from China.

Cycling Circuit

The most ambitious cycling venture ever attempted by man was undertaken by Thomas Stevens in 1884. Leaving California in April, the young San Franciscan crossed the United States on his bike, sailed for Europe, resumed his bicycle travel across Europe and Asia, and sailed across the Pacific, arriving back in San Francisco less than three years after he had set off. Stevens had actually ridden around the world on a bicycle!

THE SENTENCE BELIEVED to be the longest ever to appear in literature is found in Victor Hugo's *Les Miserables*. This sentence contains 823 words, 93 commas, 51 semicolons, and 4 dashes, and occupies almost three full pages.

THE KISS IS NOT the sole property of the human species, for actions resembling the kiss are found among a great many animals. Birds use their bills in a form of caress. Snails and certain insects caress antennae. And monkeys, of course, are extremely fond of kissing.

EARLY EUROPEAN LAMPS were always smoky, because the center of the round wick received too little air for proper combustion. But this drawback was overcome in the 18th century with the introduction of the flat-wick lamp. In that era, the most popular lamp fuel was whale oil; but by the 1840's, kerosene had come to the fore. The kerosene lamp is still in sporadic use today, where gas or electricity are not available.

Aid for the Eyes

If Benjamin Franklin could see his bifocals now, he'd never recognize them. Not the elaborate rhinestone-encrusted variety sported by some vanity fair. For his invention, Ben just stuck two different lenses—one for distance and one for close-up—on top of each other, and went out into the rain to fly his kite.

Half a millennium earlier, Roger Bacon had invented the first pair of spectacles. His discovery of the powers of convex lenses eased the eyestrain of his literate 13th-century contemporaries.

Although reading glasses improved slowly over the centuries, sufferers of astigmatism had to wait until 1827 for Sir George Airy to invent the cylindrical lens. And grapefruit-eaters had to wait until now for a pair of specs fitted with windshield-type wipers.

THERE ARE MORE individual species of insects on earth than there are men. Each year about 1,000 new species are discovered.

FEW PROFESSIONAL PERFORMERS have heard of an amateur comedy called *Aaron Slick from Punkin Crick*. But this 1919 play has been put on by small-town dramatic clubs in more than 25,000 communities and has been seen by over 10,000,000 people.

The Equine Imposter

In the early 1900's, a vaudeville act called *Hans, the Educated Horse* captivated Europe with a nag whose specialty was solving arithmetic problems. After the horse's trainer had written a question on the blackboard, the animal would tap out the answer with his feet, indicating 23, for instance, by tapping twice with his left foot and then three times with his right. Actually, the horse had been trained to respond to signals from its trainer which were so slight that they remained imperceptible for years.

THE BLUE WHALE is the largest and most powerful animal ever to have graced the planet. The largest accurately measured specimen was captured off Scotland in 1926; it measured 109 feet 4¼ inches in length. A whale caught off Argentina five years later is said to have weighed 195 tons.

IT HAS BEEN CALCULATED that in the last 3,500 years there have been only 230 years of peace throughout the civilized world.

THE ROSS SHELF ICE, an ice sheet in Antarctica, is 500 to 1,500 feet thick and covers an area the size of France.

AMONG THE MASAI TRIBESMEN of Tanzania, spitting is regarded as an indication of reverence and good will. Newborn children are spat upon by those who wish to endow the child with good luck. Masai will spit at each other when they meet, and spit at each other again to say goodbye. To seal a bargain, two traders will spit at each other.

FOR THE TEA SHIPS of 1610, sailing from the Orient to Europe was perilous. The seas swarmed with pirates and cutthroats; there were few charts to show reefs and rocks; and the frail vessels were often sunk by storms. In 1618, another method of transportation was tried—tea was brought by camel caravan from China across the deserts and mountains of Asia to Eastern Europe. The journey took 18 months.

THE FIRST EUROPEAN book mentioning tea was published in Venice in 1559. The first account of tea in English appeared in 1598 in the *Voyages and Travels* of Hugo van Linschooten, a Dutchman who had drunk tea in the far-away, mysterious Orient. Perhaps it was because of him that the Dutch were the first people in Europe to drink tea. During the 1660's, their ships carried most of the leaf to the West. In 1669, the East India Company began transporting tea to England from Java.

Swapping Spouses

The exchanging of wives is still practiced among the Eskimos, sometimes for quite practical reasons. For instance, if a man who is going on a journey has a wife encumbered with a child, he may exchange wives with a friend who is remaining in camp and therefore will not suffer any inconvenience.

Among the Himalayan mountaineers, the exchanging of wives was a common practice when two men became disgusted with their spouses and hoped thereby to effect an improved domestic arrangement.

THE SILKWORM SPINS a thread 12,000 times as long as its body. That's comparable to a six-foot man spinning a thread 15 miles long.

Water, Water Everywhere

On November 23, 1942, the S.S. Lomond, an English merchant vessel, was torpedoed in the South Atlantic. The explosion killed all but one man—25-year old Poon Lim. After being catapaulted off the deck by the blast, Lim grabbed hold of a drifting life raft and began one of the most extraordinary feats of survival in history. Lim spent 133 days on the exposed raft before being rescued, catching fish and sea gulls for his meals.

MODERN TIMEPIECES ARE ELECTRIC, self-winding, magnetic, solar-cell-powered, etc. The most accurate time-measuring device of all is the system of twin atomic hydrogen masers installed at the U.S. Naval Research Laboratory in 1964. It is accurate to within one second per 1,700,000 years.

ONE OF THE STRANGEST land vehicles ever devised was the marsh buggy, an enormous four-wheeled contraption designed by the Gulf Oil Company to traverse the treacherous Louisiana bayous in search of mineral deposits. Looking like a giant's roller skate, the marsh buggy had wheels 10 feet tall mounted on an ordinary automobile frame.

A CHINESE PRIEST in Shanghai reportedly let his fingernails grow for 27 years. The nails reached a length of 22 ¾ inches.

A Record to Hail

Some hailstones are bigger than baseballs. Most hailstones are the size of small pebbles, but occasionally some fall that are as much as 5 inches in diameter and weigh more than a pound. On July 16, 1928, in Potter, Nebraska, a huge, single hailstone fell. It tipped the scales at one and one-half pounds—the largest hailstone on record!

JOHANN HEINRICH KARL THIEME, of Aldenburg, Germany, dug an estimated 23,311 graves during his 50-year career as grave digger. In 1826, Thieme's understudy had to dig his master's grave.

RAIN KEEPS THE EARTH DRY. It is the rain process that
takes the moisture out of the air and gathers it into
concentrated rain clouds. Were it not for this, moisture
would condense on every solid surface; and all
humanity, bathed in tepid, humid perspiration, would
slide over the damp and slippery earth, like life
prisoners in a steam bath!

Pool Shark

In 1956, the great pocket billiards champion Willie
Mosconi won a tournament match against Jimmy
Moore by running the entire game—150 balls—in one
inning. Moore played a safety shot on the break, and
never got to shoot again.

The skillful Mosconi once ran 526 balls in a row—a
world's record—and won the world's championship in
1953 by running the game in only two innings.

Deep Fry

While waiting for the charcoal to turn white in your transistor-sized hibachi, it may be some consolation to consider the backyard parties of certain tribes in New Guinea. They dig a pit, 20 feet long, 15 feet deep, and 10 feet wide, burn logs in it till it's half-filled with glowing coals, and then toss in wet leaves, followed by upwards of 50 whole pigs. They cover the whole shebang with sand, and go away to dance for two days, until they hear the words so dear to all barbecue stand-bys: "C'mon and get it."

AROUND 1850, ONE Don Jose Gallegos, of Malaga, invented a musical instrument which he called the *Guitarpa*. It combined a harp, a guitar, and a violin-cello, and had 35 strings. Twenty-six strings and 21 pegs acted upon the harp. Six strings belonged to the Spanish guitar, while three silver strings and 18 pegs managed the violin-cello. The pedestal by which the instrument was supported was so constructed that the Guitarpa could be either elevated or lowered at the musician's pleasure.

THE LARGEST LAKE in the world is not called a lake, but is misnamed the Caspian Sea. Lying between Asia and Europe, it covers an area of over 43,000 square miles, and it is about four and one-half times as large as the second largest lake, Superior.

Believing in the Wind

Chicago may be the windy city, but it can't compare to Adelie Land, in the Antarctic region. The *average* wind velocity there is 50 miles an hour, and hurricanes of 100 mph or more are regular occurrences.

The highest wind velocity ever recorded in the United States was 231 mph, on Mount Washington, New Hampshire, in 1934.

AN ADULT FLATFISH—a large group of fish that includes the flounder, halibut, and sole—has both eyes on the same side of its head.

BETWEEN 1881 AND 1889, a French company attempting to construct a canal across the isthmus of Panama lost $325 million and 20,000 men before going bankrupt.

THE RECORD FOR the most strikes in a row in a sanctioned bowling match is 29. That's two-and-a-half perfect games!

Handy Andes

Tourists huffing and puffing in the cold, rarified air of the Andes Mountains often wonder how the Andean Indians can live comfortably at altitudes of up to 17,000 feet. What these tourists don't realize is that the Andean Indians are much better suited to the rigors of this climate than are other men. The lungs of these mountain inhabitants are larger, and their veins contain about two quarts more blood than those of sea-level dwellers. The Indians' slower-beating hearts are about one-fifth larger than ours, their arms and legs are shorter, and their eyes are covered with a fold of skin to keep the eyeball from freezing.

THE MOST WIDELY SPOKEN language on earth is Chinese, with 750 million speakers. English is spoken by 300 million. Russian, Spanish, Hindi, Bengali, Arabic, Japanese, German, and Portuguese complete the top ten, in that order.

BURING THE MID 1700's, two thirds of all tea drunk in England was smuggled into the country to avoid the high import tax.

AN OLD SCOTTISH CUSTOM held that a casket should be carried out of a house not through the door, but through an opening made in the side of the house and walled up immediately after the casket's departure. The belief was that a ghost could reenter a house only through the opening through which he had left it.

The Whole Story

Next to apple pie, nothing is considered more American than the doughnut. During the two World Wars, special doughnut-making machines went from one battle area to another to provide soldiers with this favorite American treat.

So it may come as quite a surprise to learn that the doughnut is not American. It was brought over from the Netherlands more than 300 years ago by the Dutch colonists, and then became a popular accompaniment to coffee and milk.

No BIRDS now on earth have teeth.

BACK IN 1927, Lawrence Grant and Dr. Munro MacLennan began a chess match at Glasgow University. The game has still not ended. The pair make one move every Christmas, and they expect a result this decade.

THE MICROPANTOGRAPH—a device used to cut extremely small markings on calibrated instruments—is capable of producing writing—legible under a microscope—on the scale of 32,000,000 words to a square inch. That's about as many words as there are in 250 300-page novels!

TERNS MIGRATE HALFWAY around the world twice each year. They summer in the Arctic, then in the autumn move south to the Antarctic region—a trip of some 11,000 miles. The next spring, they trek back to the Arctic!

According to Hoyle

Edmond Hoyle has been credited with formulating the rules to many popular games, but actually Hoyle wrote only two books on card playing. Furthermore, Hoyle never heard of most of the games for which he is supposed to have formulated the rules. Among them is poker, which was not invented until almost 100 years after Hoyle's death.

UNTIL 1869, COFFEE was the chief crop of Ceylon (now Sri Lanka). In that year, a terrible blight attacked the Ceylonese coffee trees and soon killed them all. The planters decided to start again with tea. Today, tea is the principle crop of that island.

THE U.S. PATENT OFFICE has on file a patent for boots with pockets for use by nudists.

THE EARTH DOES NOT revolve around the sun once every 365 days. Rather, it takes our planet 365 days, 5 hours, 48 minutes, and 46 seconds to make the circuit. The extra time is accounted for by the addition of an extra day once every four years—except those years divisable by 100 but not by 400.

THE TALLEST DOG extant is the Irish Wolfhound "Broadbridge Michael." Owned by a woman in Kent, England, it measures 39 1/2 inches at the shoulder.

BECAUSE THE TUNA needs a continual flow of water across its gills in order to breathe, the fish would suffocate if it ever stopped swimming.

Unhappy Firsts

The first automobile accident in the United States occurred in New York City on May 30, 1896, when a car driven by a Massachusetts man collided with a bicycle rider. The bicyclist was injured, and the driver was forced to spend the night in jail awaiting the hospital report.

The first person to die as a result of a car accident was Henry H. Bliss, a 68-year old real estate broker, who was run over as he alit from a New York City streetcar on September 13, 1899. The driver of the car was arrested.

WHISKEY IS OBTAINED through the distillation of the fermented mash of grain. It is then aged in wood. Whiskey is produced principally in the United States, Canada, Scotland, and Ireland. Scotch whiskey gets its distinctive smoky flavor due to the use of peat in drying the barley malt and also through the quality of Scotch water.

ON APRIL 14, 1910, a record 12,226 paid customers attended the opening-day ceremonies of the baseball season in Washington, D.C., and saw President William H. Taft throw out the first ball. Taft was the first President to perform the honored task, and the baseball season has traditionally begun the same way ever since.

DID YOU KNOW that when you eat tapioca pudding, you're eating a dish made from the starch of the Brazilian cassava root?

KING AUGUSTUS III of Poland boasted a wardrobe that was probably unmatched in all history. The monarch, who died in 1764, filled two entire halls with his clothes, and for each of his many costumes he had a special watch, snuffbox, cane, sword, and wig. Augustus consulted a book in which his outfits were reproduced in miniature to choose his royal apparel for the day.

IN HER LIFETIME, one termite queen can produce over 500 million children.

IN THIS CENTURY, more than 1,600 people have been publicly whipped in Delaware, where an old law provides this form of outdated punishment for the perpetrators of 24 minor crimes.

In 17th-century America, "trials by touch" were held in which the defendant in a murder case was forced to touch the body of the victim to see if the corpse "gave a sign." The belief was that if the murderer touched the body of the victim, the corpse would move or somehow indicate the individual's guilt.

The term *bootlegger* originated on the Indian reservations of the West. Since it was unlawful to sell alcoholic spirits to the Indians, ingenious peddlers often carried flasks of firewater in their boots to conceal them from government agents.

In 1869, Charles Elmer Hires opened a drug store in Philadelphia and placed a sign over his fountains which read "Hires Root Beer—5¢," thus taking the honor of manufacturing and selling the first root beer in the United States. Seven years later Hires started the national root beer business which still bears his name.

What a Card

Most authorities agree that the earliest use of cards was as much for divination as for gaming. Hindu playing cards, for instance, used 10 suits representing the 10 incarnations of Vishnu. To this day, cards remain connected with many religious rites.

How were cards introduced to Europe? Some authorities credit the Crusaders, others the Saracens, some the gypsies, and still others point to the Tartars. More than likely, all of these sources are in some part responsible, since cards appeared in many different countries during the late 14th century.

It is the Italians who are credited with the introduction of those picture cards called the Tarot. This deck consists of 22 pictorial representations of material forces, elements, virtues, and vices, one of which was the forerunner of our modern-day joker. For centuries, gypsies have been reputed to foretell the future based on the interpretation of Tarot cards, which use characters and dress strikingly similar to those of the Romany tribe.

At some point the two types of cards—the Tarot and the playing deck—were combined, resulting in a 78-card deck composed of the 56 cards of the oriental variety and the 22 of the tarot. The game derived is still popular in several countries. Further combinations of numbers and pictures resulted in decks of 40 cards (Italy and Spain), 32 cards or 36 cards (Germany), and 52 cards (France). This last deck became the standard in all English-speaking countries. The English retained the French symbols for the suits, but gave them English names. Today, if you want to call a spade a spade in France, you would say *pique*. In German, a spade is a *grun;* and in Italian, a *spada*. The costumes worn by the jack, queen, and king are of the time of Henry VII and Henry VIII.

The Soviet government attempted to substitute revolutionary figures for those of the corrupt monarchy, but the card tradition was so well entrenched that they finally had to give up.

The number of decks in circulation, long limited by the expense of hand-painting, rose dramatically with the invention of wood engraving and block printing. Today, there are more than 70 million decks sold per year in the United States alone.

THE LONGEST FIGHT in the history of boxing took place in New Orleans on April 6-7, 1893. Andy Bowen and Jack Burke fought for 110 rounds—seven hours and 19 minutes—only to have the referee break up the fight and declare it "no contest."

Jackhammer Blues

Even the largest, most well-equipped symphony orchestra in the world could not perform John Cage's *First Construction in Metal* without first scouting around for a number of additional instruments. The score for this avante-garde piece calls for, among other things, a piano with a metal rod strung across the strings, 12 oxen bells, eight cow bells, four brake drums, five thunder sheets, four Turkish cymbals, four Chinese cymbals, three Japanese temple gongs, tubular bells, sleigh bells, a tam-tam, and—from the blacksmith's shop—four muted anvils.

THE CONSTRUCTION OF the ancient megalithic formation at Stonehenge, England, required an estimated 1.5 million man-hours of labor.

THE AVOCADO HAS three singular features: (1) its protein content is greater than that of any other fruit; (2) its ripeness can be determined only by a laboratory test of its oil content; and (3) its growth is sometimes so prolific that trees have collapsed under the weight of their fruit.

Sheer Coincidence

In 1925, a staff composer for Witmark, the New York music publisher, wrote a song called "Me Neenyah." The company printed and copyrighted it at once. Soon after, copies were sent to Europe, and a music publisher in Germany informed Witmark that the song was an infringement on one which had been copyrighted in Germany in 1924. Witmark and his composer compared the two pieces and found them identical, note for note, with the exception of one half-tone. Clearly, it was a coincidence—a composer might steal a few bars but not an entire melody. The German publisher and Witmark agreed on this point, and the matter was dropped.

To DATE, WE have had only one left-handed President, James A. Garfield, and even he was subjected to the conversion attempts of his parents. Though eventually he learned how to write with his right hand, he did not abandon the use of his naturally dominant left. Legend has it that our 20th President once demonstrated his ambidextrous powers by writing Latin with one hand while he wrote in Greek with the other.

THE HEAVIEST ORGAN in the human body is the liver, which weighs an average of 3 1/2 pounds. This is more than five times the weight of the heart.

FOR GREAT OCCASIONS, nomadic Arab tribes usually prepare a feast whose main dish is, at least in size, without equal. This dish consists of eggs which are stuffed in fish, the fish then stuffed in chickens, and the chickens then stuffed in sheep, and the sheep finally stuffed in a whole roasted camel.

FOR MORE THAN 300 years, Allegri's famous "Miserere" has been sung during Holy Week in Rome's Sistine Chapel. The work was considered so sacred that, for well over a century after its completion, anyone who attempted to transcribe its score was subject to excommunication. But in 1769, a 13-year-old boy named Mozart wrote the composition down from memory after hearing it twice. Soon afterward, it was published in England. Nothing came of the Church's threat.

THE HIGHEST POINT in the conterminous United States— the 14,494-foot peak of Mount Whitney in California— can be seen from the lowest point in the nation, which lies 282 feet below sea level in Death Valley, California. The two extremes are within 100 miles of each other.

On July 31, 1964, Alvin Parker flew a single-seat glider over a distance of 644 miles—the longest single-seat glider flight on record. Not bad for a plane without a motor!

Tilt!

On June 19, 1939, the city of Atlanta enacted the first pinball legislation in the United States. The bill prohibited the use of the machines and provided for a $20 fine and a 30-day work sentence for violators.

THE EARTH'S SURFACE holds 324 million cubic miles of water. Another 2 million cubic miles of H_2O lie underground, and 3,000 cubic miles are suspended in the atmosphere.

THE WORDS *laser, radar, scuba, snafu,* and *sonar* may look like ordinary words, but in fact each began as an acronym, a word formed by joining together the first letters of the words of a phrase. The phrases represented by these acronyms are:

> Laser—Light Amplification by Stimulated Emission of Radiation
> Radar—Radio Detecting and Ranging
> Scuba—Self-contained Underwater Breathing Apparatus
> Snafu—Situation Normal All Fouled Up
> Sonar—Sound Navigation Ranging

Biographical Balderdash

For the 1886 and 1888 editions of Appleton's Cyclopedia of American Biography, the policy of the editors was to accept all material received by mail. Their trusting nature made them the unwitting prey of some practical joker who sent them at least 84 biographies of fictitious persons. These phony bios were all published, and went unnoticed until 1919, when 14 of the frauds were discovered by a librarian. This led to a search that brought to light 70 more by 1936.

THE HOANG TYPEWRITER, a device for typing in Chinese characters, has 5,700 characters on a keyboard 2 feet wide and 17 inches high.

A TWO-DAY-OLD gazelle can outrun a full-grown horse.

A Quick Game of Chess

Computer chess? Forget it. Since a chess player has about 30 moves to choose from on each turn, and his opponent has about 30 possible answers to each of these 30 moves, then there are roughly 1,000 variations to just one complete move. Each of these complete moves allows another 1,000 potential moves, and so on. Thus, a computer would have to consider about 10^{75} (1 and 75 zeroes) moves to determine the outcome of a short 25-move game. Even if the computer could calculate a million moves each second—far more than is now feasible—it would require 10^{69} seconds to complete the calculations for the game.

How long is that? Well, since the beginning of our solar system, 4.5 billion years ago, only 10^{18} seconds have elapsed.

You won't find the world's largest Gothic cathedral in any European city. An American church, the Cathedral of St. John the Divine in New York City is the world's largest place of worship built in the Gothic style. The church is 601 feet long and 320 feet across at its widest point.

Card Currency

If you've ever sat with a poker hand or a bridge hand so terrible that you've said to yourself, "Where did these cards come from?" you might be interested to know that they probably came from the Chinese, who modeled them after the currency of the T'ang dynasty.

Even before the invention of money, many societies had some form of gambling. One can almost imagine the big loser at an early Chinese all-night card game getting up and telling the boys he'd pay them just as soon as someone got around to inventing coin.

In ancient times, demand for the dye of royal purple—derived from particular shellfish and used to color the togas of the Romans—was so great that it stimulated the exploration that helped Rome build its great empire.

The longest throw in baseball history was the achievement of one Sheldon Lejeunne, who on October 12, 1910, threw a baseball a distance of 426 feet, 9½ inches. This is well over the average distance from the center-field fence to home plate!

RAINBOWS MAY BE seen at night. Lunar rainbows were observed and recorded in ancient times and are not uncommon. When the sun shines through a sheet of falling rain, it is very apt to form a rainbow. The same effect is caused, now and then, by moonlight. Even strong electric lights shining through rain and mist have caused this phenomenon.

AN ANCIENT REMEDY for toothache was to eat a mouse.

THERE IS A DIFFERENCE of 65,226 feet—approximately 12.35 miles—between the highest and lowest points on earth. Mount Everest, the highest peak, rises 29,028 feet. The Mariana Trench in the Pacific, the lowest point on earth, is 36,198 feet below sea level.

A CAR RUNS more smoothly at night or in damp weather simply because the air is cooler, not because it contains more oxygen; the amount of oxygen in the air is a constant. Cool air is more dense than warm air; and therefore, an engine takes in a greater weight of air when it is damp and chilly. This accounts for the increased power and the freedom from engine knock which so many motorists notice when they drive at night or in the rain.

JAMES W. ZAHAREE of North Dakota, using a fine pen and a microscope, printed Lincoln's Gettysburg Address on a human hair less than three inches long.

IN 1968, MRS. EMMA SMITH, a 38-year-old housewife from Nottinghamshire, England, was buried in a coffin for 101 days as a stunt at the Skegness Amusement Park. Her feat is still unmatched—by any living human being, that is.

A Spicy Story

Columbus made his journey to America seeking a short way to India in order to import spices. The spices were extremely important to Europe at a time when refrigeration was not known.

Nowadays, international trade in spices amounts to something over $170 million a year. Pepper alone normally accounts for over one-fourth of the world's total trade in spices.

THE LETTER USED MOST in the English language is *e*, followed by *t, a, i, s, o, n, h, r,* and *d*, in that order. But the letter *s* begins more English words than any other letter, far surpassing its nearest rival, the letter *c*.

MANY FIRST LADIES have smoked a cigarette now and then, but only two have smoked a pipe. The wife of Andrew Jackson, the country's seventh President, was a habitual pipe smoker, but she never got a chance to preside over the White House, briar in hand, for she died shortly after Jackson's election.

Mrs. Zachary Taylor, however, was reported to have often smoked a pipe in her days in the White House, though always in private. Shocking as this may seem today, pipe-smoking was a common enjoyment among American women at the time, especially in the Southwest.

Dolly Madison, wife of the fourth President, took her tobacco in the form of snuff.

THE LONG-DISTANCE swimming record holder must be Mihir Sen of India. In recent years, he has swum from India to Ceylon, across the Dardanelles, across the Strait of Gibraltar, and the length of the Panama Canal.

Appellation, U.S.A.

Among the curiously named towns and villages in the United States are such gems as:

    Accident, Maryland
    Ammunition Depot, Nevada
    Anvil Location, Michigan
    Battiest, Oklahoma
    Burnt Corn, Alabama
    Difficult, Tennessee
    Dime Box, Texas

Frostproof, Florida
Intercourse, Pennsylvania
King of Prussia, Pennsylvania
Mexican Hat, Utah
Ninety-Six, South Carolina
Social Circle, Georgia
Soso, Mississippi
Truth or Consequences, New Mexico
Whoopflearea, Kentucky
Young America, Minnesota

Airborne Thievery

The tropical man-of-war, or frigate bird, likes a fish dinner. But it doesn't fish in the way most birds do. Instead, it waits until another bird has done the work. Then it swoops down and beats the bird with its wings. The unlucky bird, trying to defend itself, lets go of the fish. The swift man-of-war dives, snatches the fish, and zooms away.

Sometimes this robber does its own fishing in mid-air above the ocean. It dives down and grabs flying fish when they sail above water.

HONOLULU, HAWAII, IS THE American city with the highest median family income—$12,539 in 1970. The city's nearest competitors were: San Jose, California; Seattle, Washington; and Indianapolis, Indiana. At the other end of the scale were New Orleans and Miami, where median family incomes were below $7,500.

BEFORE A BABY bird is hatched, it has a temporary tooth that enables it to break out of the egg. Full grown, a bird may have a beak strong enough to crack seeds, or long enough to snap up little creatures from the bottom of a stream.

Diamonds Are Forever?

Whether true beauty lies without or within, a jewel is a rare and a precious thing. The most precious stone today is the ruby, which after 1955 became increasingly rare as supplies from Ceylon and Burma dwindled. Carat for carat (one carat equals 200 milligrams), a flawless natural ruby of good color is more valuable than a diamond. An excellent six-carat ruby, for instance, recently brought $30,000 on the open market.

If rubies have topped diamonds in the gem hierarchy, diamonds nevertheless remain a girl's best friend. The diamond is the most durable of all gems— 90 times harder than the next hardest mineral, corundum. Commercially, the diamond is used to cut other stones.

If heated sufficiently, diamonds will burn. Although an ordinary fire will not ignite them, a blow torch will do the job easily. Diamonds are not affected until the temperature reaches from 1,400 to 1,607 degrees Fahrenheit, depending on the diamond's hardness. Such high temperatures are not common in ordinary fires, but they were achieved in the great 1906 fire which destroyed San Francisco.

THE FIRST PORTABLE TIMEPIECE was made in Nuremberg in 1504 by Peter Henlein. Because of their shape and heft, these early watches were called "Nuremberg live eggs." The first wrist-watch appeared as early as 1790. It was made by Jacquet-Droz and Leschot of Geneva.

THE FIRST AMERICAN to be honored with a monument in India was George Washington Carver, the black scientist. In 1947, the peanut growers of India unveiled a monument in Bombay to commemorate Carver's work with the versatile goober.

ABOUT 1700, A Swiss inventor mounted a windmill on a wagon. It was hoped that as the windmill wound up a huge spring, the vehicle would lope along under its own power.

THE SMALLEST BREED going is the Chihuahua. At maturity, this Mexican wonder generally weighs somewhere between two and four pounds, but some Chihuahuas tip the scales at no more than a pound.

EARLY METHODS OF trapping involved primarily the pitfall and deadfall. The pitfall was a pit covered with some flimsy material that would not bear weight; the deadfall consisted of a pit plus a weight (a log or stone) which would fall on the trapped animal. But modern trappers rely almost exclusively on spring-snapped, steel-jawed traps.

Steam Heat

Automobile enthusiasts were aghast. The world's speed record was held, not by one of their pet gasoline-powered cars, but by an automobile with a steam engine in the nose. And the honor of being first to travel faster than two miles a minute had gone to this traitorous device.

It happened in January, 1906, when the Frenchman Marriott took his steam-powered Stanley to Daytona Beach, Florida. On the sands outside Ormond, Marriott sped over a measured mile at a rate of 121.52 miles per hour!

Not until 1908 did the gasoline engine return unto its own. Then a huge Fiat named *Mephistopheles* zoomed to a new record, searing the cinders at the rate of 121.64 mph.

Lightning Strikes Twice?

Contrary to folk wisdom, lightning does strike twice in the same place, and may even strike as many as ten times in a single spot! Successive photographs of lightning flashes have been taken by engineers of the General Electric Company during electrical storms in the Berkshire Mountains of Massachusetts.

One can get an appreciable shock from an ordinary electric socket in a house wired at a voltage of 115. A single flash of lightning has been estimated to carry a charge of 100 million volts.

THE PENKNIFE WITH the greatest number of blades is the Year Knife, made by Joseph Rodgers & Sons Ltd. of Sheffield, England. Built in 1822 with 1,822 blades, the knife has continued to match the year ever since. The knife will finally run out of space for further blades in the year 2,000.

Tea Formation

Tea is grown on large estates of from 300 to 3,000 acres. The best teas grow at high altitudes, sometimes at over 6,000 feet. Many of these estates in India, Ceylon, and Indonesia are completely self-contained. They provide fully equipped factories, storehouses, housing for both manager and the native workers, and even schools for the children. Large estates have their own hospitals with native doctors in charge.

New tea seedlings are carefully planted by native workers three to five feet apart in the rich, tropical soil. Fern leaves are then spread over the plantings to protect the young growth from the sun's fierce, withering heat. The soil where the tea plants grow is kept well cultivated. Hand labor and oxen are widely used, but many of the modern estates have up-to-date cultivation equipment. Chemical fertilizers are used extensively.

If left to nature, the tea plant would grow into a tree 30 feet high. The cultivated plant, however, is kept pruned to a height of three or four feet. This provides delicate growth of leaf and makes plucking easy. Usually five years must pass before a tea plant is ready for plucking. A native girl can pluck as much as 40 pounds of leaf a day.

The fresh green leaves are brought to withering lofts and spread evenly on racks. Here, currents of warm, dry air remove a great deal of the moisture from the leaves. This process takes from 12 to 24 hours. The limp, withered leaves are rolled in special machines.

This breaks up the cells and hastens fermentation of the leaves. In the process, the leaves change color, and give out the fragrant aroma we associate with tea.

No TRAIN HAS ever run over the tracks of the Hampden Railroad, near Belchertown, Mass.

THE HIGHEST TIDES anywhere in the world are to be found in the Bay of Fundy, which separates New Brunswick from Nova Scotia. At the head of the bay, a few times each year, the tides rush in and out at a rate of 10 feet an hour—an incredible 60 feet from highest to lowest tide. The tide moves nearly as fast as the water rises in a bathtub with both taps opened full, and the rise of the tide goes on for six hours, twice a day. At no time is the water in the bay still.

ELEKTRO, THE MECHANICAL MAN, was made by the
Westinghouse Company, and first exhibited in New
York City during the World's Fair of 1939-40. The
seven-foot, 260-pound robot was set in motion by
vibrations of the human voice. He could walk, smoke,
count on his fingers up to 10, tell whether an object held
before him was red or green, and perform 20 or so other
feats. Elektro's electrical system contained 24,900 miles
of wire, or enough to encircle the globe.

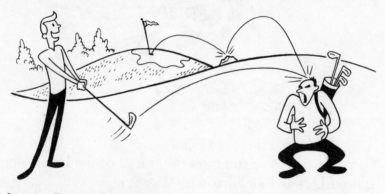

Jones Putts One Over

If you gave Bobby Jones a golfing riddle, he gave you
an answer. Long putts are the greatest problem in golf,
and Jones showed everybody how to handle them.

In 1928, for 10 consecutive rounds, Jones averaged
30 putts a round.

Confronted with the longest putt in the game—a
120-foot affair on a green at St. Andrews, Scotland—
Bobby unsheathed his putter, *Calamity Jane,* and
knocked the little white ball into the little green cup for
a world's record.

FOR ALMOST 200 YEARS, a festival called the Fiesta of the Radishes has been held each December 23 in Oaxaca, Mexico. During the festival, immense radishes are sold, and native artists carve them into many shapes— fantastic figures of men and animals. Prizes are awarded for the best and most imaginative shapes.

THE WORLD'S LARGEST GEM reposes not in a wealthy dowager's vault but in a glass case on the fifth floor of the American Museum of Natural History in New York City. A topaz of 1.38 million carats, taken from Brazil's Minas Geraes, it weighs 596 pounds. It is rather dull-looking, and few of the visitors who make it up to the fifth floor pay this huge gem any mind.

A Gift of Gulls

The pioneer people of Salt Lake City, Utah, had watched the summer sun of 1884 bring forth a good crop. They needed the food to get through the coming winter. But out of nowhere an all-consuming mass of crickets swept across the fields. The pioneers fought them in every way they knew, but the crickets kept on eating.

Suddenly, a flock of seagulls arrived to feast on the crickets, gorging themselves until all the marauders were consumed. Fortunately, enough of the crop was left to sustain the people through the winter.

The people of Salt Lake erected a monument to their unexpected saviors and passed a law prohibiting anyone from killing a seagull.

WHAT COUNTRY BOASTS the safest drivers? Surprisingly, the Philippines have the lowest traffic fatality rate of any nation, 1.5 deaths per 100,000 population. Though you might guess that the U.S. is plagued with the most reckless drivers in the world, four other countries show a worse record. Who these are is likely to surprise you— Canada, Australia, West Germany, and Austria. Austria, at the bottom of the barrel, has a rate of 31.9 traffic deaths per 100,000 population. The United States averages 26.7.

OCEAN WAVES ARE sometimes 80 feet high. Most so-called mountainous waves are only 30 to 40 feet high, and no ocean wave is higher than 100 feet from trough to crest. The highest wave ever scientifically measured was 80 feet tall. But mariners are sure some waves are as high as a ten-story building.

THE ENCHANTING ISLAND CITY of Mont-St.-Michel, a popular tourist attraction off the coast of Normandy, was actually part of the mainland of France until 725. In that year, a tremendous earthquake shook the coast and left the city surrounded by water.

As Black As Snow?

We say "as white as snow," but the Japanese, repeating the phrase on January 31, 1925, laughed; and, on December 6, 1926, the French thought of the expression and howled. For on the first date, snow fell on Japan and it was *gray;* and at the later date, snow fell in France and it was *black!*

Dr. Fujiwara, of Japan's Tokyo Observatory, explained that the odd event was due to a mixture of snow and ashes from nearby volcanoes. On the other hand, the French could offer no explanation. They just looked at the snow and shrugged their shoulders.

SIDNEY BECHET WAS the first man to play a number of musical instruments in recording a song. He used six in making *The Sheik of Araby,* released in 1941. The feat was accomplished by recording the first instrument, re-recording it while the second was played in the studio, and so on until the disc contained the parts of all six instruments—soprano sax, clarinet, tenor sax, piano, bass fiddle, and drums.

TODAY, MOST JEWELRY adorns the hands, faces, and necks of women. But in ancient Rome, men sported more baubles and bangles than their mates. In fact, unmarried Roman girls were actually prohibited by law from wearing pearls. The pearls were worn instead by young men, who placed the pearls in tiny bells which, hanging from their ears, tinkled gaily.

Now You See It, Now You Don't

Falcon Island, 2,000 miles east of Australia, has been putting on a disappearing act for the last sixty years. In 1913, the tiny island—which was actually the peak of a submarine volcano—disappeared without warning under the sea. Thirteen years later, after a series of volcanic eruptions, the island reappeared and remained a tiny part of the British Empire until 1949, when the island suddenly disappeared again.

FIVE GOLF PARTNERS teed off at the Ithaca Country Club one fine summer day in 1938, and achieved one of the most remarkable scores in the entire history of golf. Playing a short par-three hole, the five golfers posted respective scores of 1, 2, 3, 4, and 5.

THE GREATEST SINGLE RAINFALL fell in the Philippines. In 1911, from July 14 to July 17, the floodgates of heaven opened wide over Baguio, and down gushed a record 88 inches of rain—or more than *seven feet of water!*

ANYONE CAN SWIM or float more easily in salt water than in fresh water because salt water is heavier, and thus has greater buoyancy. There is so much salt in the Great Salt Lake of Utah, that one cannot sink or completely submerge oneself in it. Nevertheless, an inexperienced swimmer can drown if he panics and loses his balance. Although his body will float on the surface, the brine will suffocate him.

TRACK STAR GLENN CUNNINGHAM, for years the record-holder for the indoor mile, had a toeless left foot.

A SEVEN-INCH North African ostrich egg takes 40 minutes to boil.

Leafing Through History

Although it was Sir Walter Raleigh who smoked a bowl of tobacco before the Queen and was promptly rewarded with a dousing by a member of the court who thought Walter was burning, it was the Spanish explorers who discovered the Aztecs smoking crushed tobacco leaves in corn husks some 100 years earlier. Cigarette smoking spread rapidly to Spain, with the beggars of Seville getting credit for the first paper-wrapped variety.

Smoking didn't become popular in Northern Europe until the 1850's, when British soldiers brought Russian cigarettes back from the Crimean War. At the same time, cigarette manufacture and tobacco cultivation spread to the United States, where machinery was developed to replace the tedious hand-rolled technique.

THREE THOUSAND FEET below the sea's surface, its waters are pitch black. Not even a tiny bit of the sun's light can penetrate down more than half a mile. Sea creatures living at depths below 3,000 feet have been found to be blind or to possess their own phosphorescent "lighting system."

AMONG THE MANY THINGS that have been manufactured to coddle the owners of pets are a pair of doggie sunglasses, doggie pajamas, and for the Hassidic canine, a dog yarmulka.

Double Your Pleasure

Norman L. Manley stepped to the seventh tee at the Del Valle Country Club course at Saugus, California. The date was September 2, 1964. He hit a prodigious drive, and the ball bounced unerringly to the green and into the cup. He had scored an ace, one of the longest ones on record. But the best was yet to come. On the very next hole, the 290-yard eighth, Manley, bubbling with excitement and confidence, hit another mammoth drive. As if directed by radar, that ball landed smack in the hole! Manley had hit two holes-in-one, back to back, scoring six strokes under par for the pair.

A ROMAN GLUTTON named Arpocras once devoured four tablecloths and a broken glass at one sitting.

THE FIRST EXPLOSION of an atomic bomb took place on July 16, 1945, in a desert area near Alamogordo, New Mexico. This was only 21 days before a similar device was detonated over Hiroshima, Japan.

THE TOTAL COST of constructing the Eiffel Tower in Paris was recovered from sightseers' fees during the first year after the Tower's completion.

OUNCE FOR OUNCE, the tiny shrew is the most ferocious of all mammals. This tiny creature kills and eats twice its weight in food every day.

THE WHITE DWARF star A.C. 70 8247 is about 36 million times as dense as water. One cubic inch of matter from this star would wiegh 650 tons. If a water pitcher were filled with such matter, the weight of the pitcher could not only collapse a table, but the floor under it—and the whole building as well.

THE PENTAGON IS the largest office building in the world, with a total floor area of 6-1/2 million square feet. Yet no two offices in the building are more than 1,800 feet—or six minutes walking time—distant from each other.

The Rain in Spain

Sometimes, in Europe, the rain is red. The so-called "blood rains" of Europe used to plunge the people of that continent into a frenzy. The scientific cause of the phenomenon was not known, and the pinkish rain was thought to be diluted blood.

There are still "blood rains" at odd intervals in Italy, southern France, and southeastern Europe. It seems that storms lift reddish desert dust from the Sahara, and blow billions of these particles across the Mediterranean into the cloudbanks above Europe. Then they are washed down as red rain.

THE CIRCUMFERENCE OF THE EARTH is about 42 miles greater around the equator than it is around the poles.

BATS ARE NOT BLIND, but their vision is extremely poor. These winged mammals actually fly by radar, emitting high-pitched sounds from their throats and picking up the echoes with their super-sensitive ears.

IN 1946, CASTING for distance, Wilbur Brooks of Indianapolis set his toe in the dirt, took a deep breath, and sent ⅝ of an ounce of bait 427 feet for a world's record. Out Wilbur's way the fish never knew what hit them!

An Arboreal Affair

Among the Brahmans of southern India, a younger brother may not marry before an older one. When there is no bride available for the senior brother, he is often married to a tree, which leaves the younger brother free to take a wife. Sometimes the tree marriage takes place at the same time as the regular marriage, in the belief that some evil influence which would otherwise attach to the newly wedded pair will be diverted to the tree.

THE LARGEST JIGSAW puzzle in the world, made in 1954, measured 15 feet by 10 feet and contained over 10,000 pieces.

YOUNG PUFFINS ARE FED and fed until they grow larger than their overworked parents. Then their parents fly away. The youngsters are too fat to start food-searching on their own, but well larded as they are, they don't starve. They live off their stored fat, gradually getting thin enough to go out on their own.

Barnum's Biggest Star

In 1882, Jumbo—the largest elephant ever seen in captivity—was sold by the London Zoo to P.T. Barnum. A loud cry of protest immediately arose from the elephant's English admirers—who included Queen Victoria in their numbers. But the protest was to no avail—the elephant sailed to America with a deluge of gifts sent by his English friends. The gargantuan pachyderm—to which we owe the term "jumbo"—was part of Barnum's circus until the elephant was killed by an express train in Canada in 1885.

BEFORE EATING ANYTHING, a raccoon will first wash the food in the nearest available water. Some raccoons will go hungry rather than eat unwashed food; others will go through the motions of washing when there is no water around.

SCIENTISTS AT THE U.S. Air Force Missile Development Center at Holloman, New Mexico, constructed a train that traveled so fast that no human could ride in it. The rocket-powered sled attained a speed of 3,090 mph on a 6.62-mile-long rail track.

THAT ST. PATRICK drove all snakes from Ireland is certainly a legend, but the truth is there are no native snakes on the island. Other islands without native serpents include Crete, New Zealand, Malta, Iceland, and Hawaii.

It Never Rains, It Pours

New York City, with an average annual rainfall of 43 inches, is pretty bad. Foggy London has only 25, and sunny Los Angeles gets by with 15. Bergen, Norway, seems wet indeed with 73 inches. But Bergen is dry as a desert compared with Cherrapungi, India, which has an annual downpour of 432 inches, or 36 feet!

THE SPOON AS we know it today, with its spatulate handle, dates from only the 18th century.

THE HEAVIEST WEIGHT ever lifted by a human being is 6,270 pounds, accomplished by Paul Anderson at Toccoa, Georgia, in 1957. The 5-foot, 10-inch strongman, using his back, lifted a table loaded with a lead-filled safe and heavy auto parts. The weight of the objects equalled that of a 33-man college football team!

OF ALL MAN-MADE structures on earth, the only one that might conceivably be visible from the moon is the Great Wall of China.

Spilling the Beans

Intent on preserving a monopoly, the Dutch forbade taking coffee seedlings from their East Indian plantations. But a dashing young Brazilian officer won the heart of the wife of the governor of Dutch Guiana, a coffee growing colony in South America, and as a token of her affection, she gave him some of the precious beans and cuttings, anticipating Cole Porter by declaring her love thusly: "Take the beans, for you're the cream in my coffee!"

IN THE 19TH century, students at Cambridge University, England, were not permitted to keep a dog in their rooms. Lord Byron, the famed poet, complied with the rule—he kept a bear instead.

THE FIRST BUILDING erected by the American Government in Washington, D.C. was the Executive Mansion, designed by James Hoban and modeled after the palace of the Duke of Leinster in Ireland. Construction began in 1792, and the building was first occupied by President John Adams in 1800. The mansion was burned by the British in 1814 but later restored, with all stones painted white to obliterate evidence of the blaze. Since that time, the building has been known as the White House.

Slumberland

How much sleep does one need? Answer: Anywhere from five to ten hours. Science has come up with no explanation as to why one individual requires more sleep than another. An infant sleeps most of the day because he is growing at a faster pace than at any other period in his life.

As we age, the quality of our sleep tends to gradually deteriorate. The sleep of older people is sometimes so fragmented that it is little more than a series of catnaps. Winston Churchill managed to turn his handicap into an advantage. He took short snoozes throughout the day to rejuvenate himself; and he insisted that his daily nap in the afternoon turned one day, in effect, into two. Still, medical evidence suggests that sustained sleep is more helpful; "to sleep like a baby" is an apt description of ideal slumber.

However, not even the sleep of infants is always tranquil. In the 1950's, psychologists Eugene Aserinsky and Nathaniel Kleitman observed a regular pattern in the sleep of infants: intervals of quiet slumber alternated with periods of body activity. Extending their discovery to a study of adult sleep, these scientists noticed recurring periods of rapid eye movements (*REMs*) beneath the closed lid, alternating with periods of peaceful sleep. These REMs, the psychologists learned, signaled the onset of dreams.

The Weight of Responsibility

On May 20 of each year, a ceremony known as the Weighing of the Mayor takes place in High Wycombe, England. Outside the town hall, the mayor, his wife, and a number of minor officials are each placed on the scales and their weights are announced to the assembled populace, along with the weights of the previous year's incumbents.

SINCE THEIR FORMATION 10,000 years ago, the Niagara Falls have eaten their way seven miles upstream. If they continue at that rate, they will disappear into Lake Erie in 22,800 years.

THE ROYAL SOCIETY for the Prevention of Accidents erected a display stand at the Institute of Personnel Management Conference in Harrowgate, England. It collapsed.

Amphibious Assault

It sometimes rains frogs. Scientists explain the phenomenon of raining frogs in this way: Spawn are sucked up from rivers and lakes into the atmosphere by whirlwinds. The lightweight embryos are carried through the air for great distances. The spawn hatch en route. When the wind is spent, the animals drop to the earth!

SINCE THE 19TH CENTURY, the *Tour d'Argent*—the oldest restaurant in Paris—has given a memento ticket to every diner who orders the specialty of the house, *canard rouennais*. The name and number of the guest is entered in a visitors' book, a unique record which has now reached six figures. Ticket number 112,151 went to President Franklin D. Roosevelt; 203,728 to Marlene Dietrich; and 253,652 to Charlie Chaplin.

A Rude Shock

In 1864, an Australian named Siegfried Marcus was experimenting with the lightbulb, and he wasn't very successful. He ignited a mixture of gasoline and air, believing he would at last be producing illumination. He was right. But he also produced a violent explosion, jolting him into the discovery that his mixture could be a method of powering a vehicle. The drawback, however, was that his contraption required a strong man to lift the rear end of the vehicle while the wheels were being spun to get the engine going. Like almost all inventors, Marcus was a bit crazy; and after 10 years, he lost interest in the automobile, calling it "a senseless waste of time and effort."

By this time, the steam vehicle was already coming under public pressure because of the noise it engendered. Moreover, the steam engine was considered downright dangerous, and so it was common for early motorists to find the roadway blocked with barricades.

AT MANY A FIESTA held in rural Mexico, one of the treats enjoyed by the guests is ant candy. This unusual confection consists of the bodies of ants which gather honey from a species of oak leaf. The ants swell enormously until they are about the size of gooseberries. After the ants' legs and heads are removed, their bodies are piled on dishes and served as candy. The taste of these insects is very similar to that of a sweet, juicy fruit.

THE NEXT TIME your day at the beach is ruined by cloudy skies, just remember this: without clouds and the other constituents of the earth's atmosphere, the surface of our planet would reach a temperature of 176 degrees at the equator by day, and -220 degrees at night!

Executive Excursions

The first President to ride in an automobile was Theodore Roosevelt, but he didn't much care for it and seldom allowed the Secret Service chauffeur to take him out for a spin.

The next President, William Howard Taft, made more regular use of his brougham, but he didn't drive the car himself—perhaps because his enormous girth would not allow him to squeeze beneath the steering wheel.

Warren G. Harding was the first man elected President who drove a car himself.

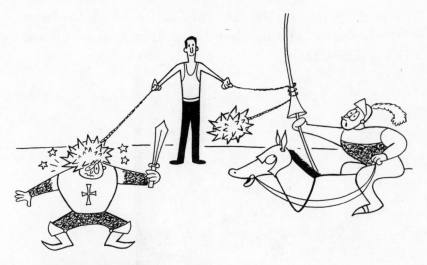

A Deadly Device

The mace is a shafted weapon held in one hand. It employs a flail at the end of a chain. The flail, or spiked ball, is linked to a wooden handle by the chain. While it cannot be snapped like a whip, the mace is wielded in much the same fashion. It was possible to envelop the opponent's sword blade with the chain, and thus to pull his weapon from his hand, or to knock the enemy senseless within his armor with the mace. One could even crush his skull.

In England, this weapon was called a *Morning Star*. In Spain, it was called a *mate suegra* or "mother-in-law killer." Originally a farmer's thresher, the mace became, as so many tools did, a peasant's weapon. Spikes were added to the ball to make it more effective. The length of chain made it easier to swing it about, and clear a path through a wall of armor.

THE INVENTION OF the first mechanical clock has been attributed to I'Hsing and Liang Ling-tsan of China, circa 725 A.D.

KING PRAJADHIPOK, ruler of Siam from 1925 until 1935, took out unemployment insurance policies with European companies to insure himself against the loss of his throne. He was forced to abdicate in 1935 and lived comfortably on the insurance money until his death in 1941.

NOT ALL ICEBERGS are white. Vegetable matter frozen into a berg can give the massive ice floe a green or black color.

ON DECEMBER 19, 1922, Mrs. Theresa Vaughn was brought before a police court in Sheffield, England, on a charge of bigamy. During the hearing, the 24-year-old Mrs. Vaughn not only admitted to the charge, but confessed to having married 61 other men over a period of five years—without obtaining a divorce from any one of them.

YOU'LL NEED MORE THAN a set of strong glasses to read the copy of Omar Khayyam's *Rubaiyat* in the Bodelian Library at Oxford University—you'll need a microscope! This book—the smallest in the world—is only one-quarter inch high and three-sixteenths of an inch wide, and weighs just 1/327 of an ounce.

Phony Figures

As of 1970, 120.2 million telephones were in use in the United States alone, considerably more than the combined number of phones in Japan, Great Britain, West Germany, Russia, and Canada. Out of 100 households in New York State, 95 had telephones. And Washington, D.C., averaged 102 telephones per hundred households!

The state that has been best able to resist the lure of electronic gab is Mississippi, which has only 75 phones per 100 households—still a fantastic proportion when compared to even the most technologically advanced nations of the world. For example, Japan has less than 40 phones per 100 households, and West Germany has less than 35 per 100.

WOMEN AS YOUNG AS six and as old as 62 have become mothers, while men as young as 13 and as old as 100 have become fathers.

THE FASTEST TRAIN in the world is the Japanese National Railroad's Hikari run, between Kyoto and Nagoya. The Hikari makes the 83-mile trip in only 47 minutes, for an average speed of 106.5 miles per hour.

ON JANUARY 15, 1919, a tank containing 2,000,000 gallons of molasses exploded in Boston, killing 21 persons and injuring 50. Many of the victims were literally drowned in molasses.

GAZELLES, PRAIRIE DOGS, wild asses, and many other animals never drink water. They have a special chemical process which transforms a part of their solid food into water.

The Fire Extinguished by an Iceberg
The fateful voyage of the British liner *Titanic* was marred by disaster from the very beginning. As the 46,000-ton vessel left its dock in Southhampton on April 10, 1912, a fire broke out in a bunker. Four days later, when the mammoth liner struck an iceberg and went down in the North Atlantic, the fire was still burning.

THE LARGEST CLAMS in the world weigh close to 500 pounds.

WHEN THE RACEHORSE Mill Reef broke a leg, he received sympathy cards from his admirers at the rate of 30 a day.

A HUMAN BEING sheds skin continually, replacing it with an entire new outer layer once every 28 days.

A MINIATURE MODEL can be made of anything in the universe—except the universe itself. Why? If the earth were represented by a ball only one inch in diameter, the nearest star—*Alpha Centauri*—would have to be placed 51,000 miles away.

SOME CICADAS live underground for 17 years, then emerge for a few weeks of sunshine before dying.

AN AGE-OLD MYTH held that certain precious gems could produce offspring. Pearl divers in Borneo often placed a pair of pearls together in the hope that the two gems would mate and have a family.

BABIES HAVE BEEN KNOWN to hiccup several hours before birth. In some instances an unborn baby has cried loudly enough to be heard from 25 feet away.

Tea Lore
The usual tea sold in the supermarket is a blend of 20 to 30 different varieties, each chosen for a certain characteristic—color, flavor, bouquet, body.

There are three different types of tea—black, green and oolong. All three types come from the same tea bushes. It's how the leaves are processed after they are picked that makes the teas different.

Over 97 percent of all the tea consumed in the United States is black tea. In the processing, the tea is fully fermented.

Green tea is light in color when brewed. In its processing, it is not fermented at all.

Oolong tea is a compromise between black and green tea. It is semi-fermented, so that the leaves turn greenish brown.

HEBREW HAD BEEN a dead language for 2,300 years before it was revived by the Jews in Israel as their common language. There is no other case in which a dead language has been resurrected.

Low-down on the Atlantic

The greatest mountain range lies under the sea. This is known as the Dolphin Rise and extends from the Arctic to the Antarctic. Mountain tops are so high that at points they rise above the ocean's surface. We know some of these points as the Azore Islands and the Canary Islands. The deepest valleys between these mountains are, in some places, more than five miles below the surface of the ocean. If Mt. McKinley, Alaska, the highest mountain in North America, were dropped into such a spot, it would be completely submerged!

THOUSANDS OF ONE-FINGER piano pieces were written during the 19th century, and served as parlor entertainment. But *Chopsticks* is the only one of these compositions that remains popular today. Published in Glasgow in 1877, this commonplace little tune has been borrowed by such outstanding composers as Liszt and Rimski-Korsakov.

The Light Fantastic

The first electric lamp was the arc lamp, developed from the electrochemical principle demonstrated by Humphrey Davy in 1801. In 1879, Cleveland, Ohio, became the first city to use the new carbon-arc street lamps devised by C. F. Brush. Although an impracticable incandescent electric lamp appeared as early as 1858, it was not until 1879 that this type of illumination was perfected by Thomas A. Edison.

Neon lamps were invented by Georges Claude in 1911, and came into wide use within a decade. Different colors could be obtained by using different gases—argon for blue, neon for red, helium for yellow, carbon dioxide for white; and these gases could be mixed to produce virtually any color.

AN UNUSUAL BIRD indeed is the hoatzin, a rare South American species with no close relatives. A crested bird smaller than a pheasant, the hoatzin dines on leaves. But the strangest thing about this bird is that the young have claws on their *wings* in addition to those on their feet. These claws help the baby hoatzins climb about in the trees.

ON JULY 26, 1955, Ted Allen set a world's record for horseshoe pitching by throwing 72 consecutive ringers.

THE LARGEST OPERATIONAL TELESCOPE in the world is a 236.2-inch reflecting telescope in the Caucasus Mountains of the U.S.S.R. Assembled in October 1970, it is 80 feet long, weighs 935 tons, and contains a mirror which weighs 78 tons by itself. The light-gathering power of this telescope is so great that it can detect the light of a single candle, 15,000 miles away.

The range of this gargantuan instrument encompasses the entire observable universe.

The Most Fortunate Jailbird

The city of St. Pierre, on the Caribbean island of Martinique, was completely destroyed within three minutes when Mt. Pelee erupted on May 8, 1902. Of the city's 30,000 inhabitants, only one man was found alive—he'd been locked up in a deep underground jail cell.

THE LONGEST RECORDED drive of all time is 445 yards, achieved by E.C. Bliss in 1913. Playing on the Old Course at Herne Bay, Kent, England, Bliss—a 12-handicap player—put all of his 182 pounds behind his swing and sent the ball flying over a quarter of a mile. There was a 57-foot drop over the course of the drive. On that particular day, Bliss was blessed with luck, for a registered surveyor was on the scene to accurately measure his shot forthwith.

THE ANCIENT INCAS of Peru were masters at decorating their teeth. Unlike primitive tribesmen today who often grind their teeth down to fine points, the Incas inlaid their teeth with gold and semi-precious jewels. When an Inca maiden smiled, it was a very bright smile indeed. The custom was adopted briefly in the west; some wealthy women, who had more diamonds than they knew what to do with, inserted genuine sparklers in their front teeth.

GLASS, THOUGH IT feels hard enough to be called a solid, is actually a liquid. If left standing in one position, the particles that make up glass will flow downward.

Time for Tea

It is believed the first shipment of tea to the United States arrived in New Amsterdam about 1650. At the time, tea cost from $30 to $50 a pound, and in addition to making a refreshing drink, the used leaves were sometimes salted and eaten with butter.

Tea traveled with the pioneers who explored and settled our vast land. No wagon train headed West without a good supply of tea on board. Then, as now, it was the drink for people on the go who needed a lift that relaxes and refreshes.

Today the United States is the second largest consumer of tea in the world, surpassed only by Great Britain. We are the only country that prepares large quantities of tea using three different types: loose, teabags and instant.

THE EGYPTIAN PLOVER has worked out a mutually satisfactory arrangement with the crocodile: the bird gets food and the crocodile gets service. The plover rides on the crocodile's back and serves as a lookout, emitting shrill cries when danger seems imminent. The plover also digs parasites out of the crocodile's back. When the crocodile finishes its dinner, the big reptile opens up its mouth so that its small helper can hop inside, and pick its teeth clean of uneaten food.

What a Catch!

It was Saturday, April 17, 1937. The papers reported that the Wagner Labor Relations Act had been upheld by the Supreme Court, that President Roosevelt was shaping a new fiscal plan to avoid a tax rise, that Minsky's had been fined $500 in a strip-tease case, and that the first "Flying Fortress" was nearing completion in Seattle. On that same bright and sunny morning, four fishermen set out from Dallas. According to their own allegation, they too made history.

It seems that when they got into a small boat on the Dallas dock, they were determined to catch themselves some of the giant tarpon that lounge around the Gulf of Mexico. Out they sailed, far beyond the jetties, out to the sea where the tarpon run. There they settled down, let out their lines, and got all slouched in for a good bull session. These here tarpon don't bite so quick so that a coupla gents can't set back with a good cigar and take it easy-like, and—

Strike! One of the boys was practically jerked out of his seat as he whipped everyone to attention. The other 3 hurriedly began to reel in their lines to get out of his way. But it wasn't exactly free reeling. It was darn tough pulling, for each fisherman found *his own line* hooked up to a tugging tarpon.

The four Texans landed their four babies one after the other, each fish within a minute of the other. They could hardly believe what had happened. And if they couldn't, who would?

So they quickly sailed ashore and betook themselves to a notary, who for a proper fee, memorialized the day by certifying that this was "the most remarkable fishing expedition in the annals of Southern waters!"

And that's that!

THERE ARE APPROXIMATELY two and one-half times as many cattle in Argentina as there are people.

MARY MALLON, KNOWN AS "Typhoid Mary," was blamed for spreading typhoid to at least 1,300 people in New York City in 1903 alone. Despite her illness, Miss Mallon refused to stop working and often obtained jobs—under assumed names—that involved the handling of food. To prevent further contamination of the populace, "Typhoid Mary" was placed in permanent detention in 1915 and remained there until her death in 1938.

OF ALL NATIONS in the world, New Zealand has the highest rate of calorie consumption per person, as well as the highest rate of protein consumption per person. The world's greatest cereal consumers are the people of Turkey; the greatest potato and root flour consumers are the people of Paraguay; of sugar, Colombia; of alcohol, South Africa.

BEARDS WERE ONCE placed under government control in Rumania. Whiskers could be worn only if the owner secured an official permit, and paid the appropriate fee.

THE EARLY KINGS of France stuck three hairs plucked from their beards in the seal of official papers to lend the documents greater sanction.

TEQUILA, INDIGENOUS TO Mexico, is obtained from the heart-sap of the mescal cactus.

Fancy Footwear

The earliest form of shoe was the sandal, worn in ancient Egypt, Greece, and Rome. Next came the boot, generally worn for hunting and traveling, until the Romans took to wearing boots for ordinary outdoor activity.

Though the sabot had been in use much earlier, by the 11th century wooden clogs became the standard footwear of the European peasant. In the 1400's, people began to mount their shoes on separate wooden blocks to protect their footwear from mud and water. Soon, both the platform and the shoe were combined, to become the forerunner of the heeled shoe.

It was not long before Europe's fashion designers went to work. Among the more bizarre footwear developed were shoes with points so long that they had to be fastened at the knee; platform shoes with soles a foot high; shoes which were extraordinarily wide at the toes; and boots faced with fur.

Yet shoes are more outrageously styled today than they have been in centuries. Witness silver lamé shoes with Cuban heels for men; platform shoes with six-inch heels for women, and women's boots in every color of the rainbow. We've even been told of a pair of women's heels which are made of clear, hollowed-out plastic, and are filled with water and live goldfish—to create a walking aquarium.

THE BIG FISH FIGHT, and fight hard, so game fishing is usually considered a man's sport. But on May 6, 1950, Mrs. H.A. Bradley took her boat out to Cape Charles, Virginia, and brought to gaff the largest drum fish ever caught—an 87-pound, 8-ounce giant!

The Icebox of the World
The lowest temperature ever recorded was 90 degrees below O Fahrenheit, in the Siberian city of Verkhoyansk. At this temperature, ice is like stone, and snow is as hard as table salt. A person who stood still outside for five minutes without proper clothing would become a stonelike corpse. Rubber would crack as easily as glass, and mercury would turn as hard as steel.

Although no one would choose Verkhoyansk for a winter vacation, the city's climate has certain unquestionable advantages. It is virtually impossible to contract a cold or a germ-caused disease, because the air is too cold for the germs to live. And food can be stored at this low a temperature for years without spoiling.

OSTRICHES FEED UNHATCHED EGGS to their young. Several female ostriches often lay their eggs in a single nest during the mating season. They add a few each day until there is a total of two dozen. Some of these eggs hatch earlier than others. To feed their hungry babies who cannot eat the rough food of the adult ostrich, the parent birds crack open the unhatched eggs and feed them to their youngsters.

THE LONGEST BICYCLE ever constructed was a tandem bike that could seat 10. The machine was 23 feet long and weighed 305 pounds.

ON DECEMBER 8, 1959, a travelogue of China entitled *Behind the Great Wall* was presented in New York City, earning the distinction of being the first movie to be shown with accompanying scent. The scent was forced through vents in the ceiling.

WE ARE PUT to no end of trouble by a 10-inch snowfall— traffic is snarled, electricity fails, drains overflow, roofs leak. Imagine how the people of Tamarack, California, must have felt in the winter of 1906-7 when 884 inches of snow fell in one heap. That's 73 feet, a world's record.

THERE IS ONE FAMILY of birds whose young can fly immediately after being hatched. These birds are the mound builders, natives of Australia and some South Sea islands, which emerge from the shell fully feathered.

To COMMEMORATE HIS 700th parachute jump, British Army Sergeant Hector Macmillan made a leap in full Scottish national dress, including kilts, while playing *The Road to the Isles* on his bagpipes.

THE FIRST PERSON to go over Niagara Falls in a barrel was Anna Edson Taylor, who on October 24, 1901, took the plunge over Horseshoe Falls in a barrel four and a half feet high and three feet in diameter. The inside of the barrel was filled with cushions, and the passenger was harnessed inside the barrel. It was later discovered that Anna couldn't swim.

No Soap

The ancients are believed to have washed themselves
with ashes and water, which was followed by an
application of oil or grease to relieve the irritation
caused by the ashes. The first mention of soap, as we
know it today, was made in the first century A.D. by
Pliny, who wrote that some Germanic tribes washed
their hair with a mixture of tallow and ashes of wood.

Subsequently, soap became popular in Rome, but
fell into decline when the Roman Empire fell in 476.
Some 300 years later, soap was "re-discovered" by the
Italians.

Oddly enough, soap did not reach France until the
early 13th century. For many years, the English—like
the French—favored perfumes as a means of, if not
keeping themselves clean, at least seeming to. But by
the 17th century, soap became common in England,
and in its North American colonies as well. In colonial
America and Canada, many housewives made their
own soap from waste animal fats and lye.

Although soap may be made of many substances,
all methods of manufacture are based on the same
principle. Fats and oils are heated, an alkali introduced,
and the mixture stirred. When salt is added, the brew
forms a curd which floats to the top. This curd is the
soap. To produce a purer soap, the curds may be
washed with a salt solution and allowed to settle. The
upper layer thus formed is the pure soap, which is then
churned, perfumed, colored, poured into huge frames,
cut, shaped, and stamped.

QUITO, CAPITAL OF ECUADOR, sits almost directly on top of the equator. But because the city is 9,300 feet above sea level, it enjoys a spring-like climate all year around.

THE TERM *pekoe* refers only to a size of tea leaf—and not to a type or variety of tea. Other names of sizes are *Orange Pekoe, Souchong, Broken Pekoe, Fannings,* and *Dust.*

THE FIRST BOOK manuscript in the United States to be written with a typewriter was *The Adventures of Tom Sawyer*, by Mark Twain. It was typed on a Remington in 1875, but Twain did not publicize the fact that he had used the typewriter for fear he would be questioned about the operation of the machine.

Polly Want a Cracker!
The size of a parrot's vocabulary depends upon a variety of factors: the patience and perseverance of the trainer; the age at which the parrot is trained; and of course, the talent of the individual bird. Well-trained birds can accumulate a vocabulary of a few hundred words, but several birds have been taught to utter fairly complex sentences or passages.

There have been fairly reliable reports that a certain parrot was trained to recite the Lord's Prayer entire. According to the United States Biological Survey, there is no reason to doubt the claim on biological grounds.

VODKA IS AN unaged spirit obtained from potatoes or grain. It is then filtered through vegetable charcoal. In the United States, this process produces a liquid that must be "without distinctive character, aroma, or taste," but which packs quite a noticeable wallop at over 190 proof.

Strange Interlude

The shortest reign of any monarch on record was that of Louis XIX of France, whose tenure in royal office lasted but 15 minutes. On August 2, 1830, at Rambouillet, the Dauphin Louis Antoine technically became King Louis XIX upon the signature of the former king, Charles X, on an act of abdication. Fifteen minutes later, Louis signed another act of abdication, turning his crown over to Henri V.

IN URUGUAY, DUELLING is legal as long as both parties in the dispute are registered blood donors.

ON JUNE 6, 1896, George Samuelson and Frank Harpo left New York harbor in an 18-foot rowboat. Fifty-six days later they arrived on the Scilly Islands off the coast of England, thus becoming the first men to row across the Atlantic Ocean—a feat everyone thought was impossible.

THE HEAVIEST DOG on record was a Wisconsin Saint Bernard who at age five weighed 295 pounds.

The Best of Both Worlds

The Caudron company of France once devised an airplane-automobile with foldable wings. It was an entirely conventional airplane except for a small outboard motor mounted on a rear third wheel. In March, 1935, a writer for the *Scientific American* declared that he "saw no reason why some day such a combination should not be practicable for general use." But the "aviocar," as it was called, took a few trial spins down the boulevards of Paris, and that was the end of that.

How DID THE TERM *o'clock* originate? Unquestionably, the original form was *of the clock; o'clock* is merely a contraction. Many writers of the 16th and 17th centuries said *ten of clock* or *ten a clock*. In the early 18th century, the form *o'clock* began to appear.

A Golfer's Nightmare

Can you believe that a woman golfer—and not a novice either—took 166 strokes on a single hole? Well, it happened. In 1912, in the qualifying round of the Shawnee Invitational for Ladies in Pennsylvania, a poor female who shall remain nameless teed off at the 130-yard 16th hole. Her drive flew directly into the Binniekill River. With the ball floating insolently in the water, she set out in a rowboat to continue play, with her husband at the oars. After flailing away for what must have seemed an eternity, she finally drove the ball to dry land. Unfortunately, the thing landed in a dense wood and again she hacked away for what seemed forever to extricate it from the woods, into the rough, into the sand, into the rough. Before this nightmarish hole was played out, the poor woman had taken 166 strokes, all meticulously recorded by her loving husband.

RAIN NEVER FALLS on parts of the Sahara Desert. Though clouds pass over these areas, and raindrops actually fall, the water itself never reaches the ground. The sizzling heat of the desert air evaporates the moisture as it falls, changing it back to invisible vapor.

A DEVICE PATENTED in the U.S. on May 19, 1896, claimed to "produce dimples on the human body or to nurture and maintain dimples already existing."

One Man Band

A certain Austrian by the name of Karl Waetzel, who lived during the last century, had a particularly inventive turn of mind. He built a fabulous conglomeration of musical instruments which he called the *panomonico,* an instrument which could be played by a single person. The panomonico included 150 flageolets, 150 flutes, 50 oboes, 18 trumpets, 5 fanfares, three drums, and two kettledrums. The whole thing totaled 378 instruments. Waetzel's fantastic invention was purchased by Archduke Charles of Austria. The irony was that the Duke used the panomonico not to produce beautiful music, but for the purpose of annoying noisy courtiers of his royal household.

THE LONGEST-NAMED LAKE in the world is Lake Chargogagogmanchaugagogchaubunagungamaug, near Webster, Massachusetts, known locally as Lake Webster. The name, of Indian origin, means "You fish on your side, we fish on our side, nobody fishes in the middle."

THE SHORTEST WAR on record was fought in 1896 between England and Zanzibar. From the beginning of hostilities to the surrender of Zanzibar by Sultan Said Khalid, there elapsed only 38 minutes.

IN 1871, A BOOK entitled *Rosicrucian Dream Book* was published in Boston, containing the solutions to over 3,000 different dreams in alphabetical order. According to this work, a dream about potatoes indicates that someone is poisoning the minds of those who do you good. And camels in a dream mean that one's love is far better than he or she looks.

A Concert of Swine

The musical highlight of the Great Exhibition of 1851, in England, was an instrument called the pigtail organ. The organist of this most unusual instrument had assembled a herd of pigs, each of which had a squeal of a different pitch. The tails of the melodic swine were connected to a system of pincers, which were operated by the keys of the organ. To play the instrument, the organist merely pressed the desired keys and—*voilà!*— the pigs squealed out a melody, to the delight of the audience.

THE SMALLEST OF ALL BIRDS is the bee hummingbird which is about 2¼″ long, most of that length being the beak. It takes 18 of these creatures to tip the scale of one ounce.

ACCORDING TO LEGEND, Henry I of England established the yard as the distance from the point of his nose to the end of his thumb when his arm was outstretched.

THE FEMALE CUCKOO of Europe searches out the egg-filled nest of some hard-working bird and lays her single egg in that nest. Then the cuckoo picks up one of the eggs of its host, drops that egg to the ground, and flies away, never to return, hoping that the substitution won't be noticed. If the returning mother recognizes the strange egg as an interloper, she jabs a hole in it, and rolls it out of the nest.

WHAT DOES IT MEAN when the weatherman says that one inch of rain fell in your area yesterday? For instance— say one inch of rain fell on one acre of ground. Since an acre equals 43,560 square feet, a rainfall of one inch over this area would produce 6,272,640 cubic inches of water, or 3,630 cubic feet of water. A cubic foot of water weighs about 62.4 pounds, the exact weight varying with the water's density. Therefore, one inch of rain over one acre of surface would equal 226,512 pounds, or better than 113 tons of liquid.

Is a Spice an Herb?

What is a spice? According to Christopher Morley, *spice* might be the plural of "spouse." According to Webster, a spice is an aromatic vegetable such as pepper, cinnamon, nutmeg, mace, allspice, ginger, cloves, or such, used to season food and to flavor sauces and pickles.

An herb, on the other hand, is defined as "a seed plant which does not develop a woody tissue as that of a shrub or tree, but is more or less soft or succulent." An herb may be used for medicinal purposes; or because of its scent or flavor, for culinary purposes.

There is but a thin line of distinction between an herb and a spice.

In ancient times, spices were used for incense, for embalming preservatives, as ointments, as perfumes, as antidotes against poisons, as cosmetics, and for medicinal use.

OF THE MORE THAN 110 species of mammals that have become extinct in the last 1,900 years, at least 70 percent have died out within the last century. About 600 other mammal species are presently endangered and will also perish unless measures are taken now to preserve them.

THE FIRST DINING ESTABLISHMENT to print a menu offering a variety of foods and liquors was Boulanger's Restaurant, which opened in Paris in 1765. Previously, coffee houses and taverns served "Ordinaries," regular meals at a common table at a fixed time and price. Parisians so enjoyed eating when and what they liked that, 50 years later, the city had more than 125 restaurants—one of which served 197 differently prepared meat dishes!

A Careful Decision

In 1844, when Amos Lovejoy and Francis Pettygrove were laying out a new city in what is now the state of Oregon, they could agree upon everything but the choice of a name for their embryonic town. Lovejoy, a Massachusetts native, opted for Boston; Pettygrove, a former Maine resident, held out for Portland. So, the two men did the sensible thing: they flipped a coin. Pettygrove won—and the city was named Portland forevermore.

CORN IS BY FAR the biggest farm crop in the United States. Over 5 billion bushels of corn were produced in 1972, more than three times the production of the next biggest crop, wheat.

IN 1969, a poll taken in Morocco revealed that only 88 percent of those asked knew that a man had set foot on the moon. Of these, more than half thought the story was a hoax.

THE BODY OF the average adult contains 2,800 square inches of skin, making the skin the largest single organ in the human body.

ALMOST EVERY ROOM of every house in the Sahara city of El Oued, Algeria, is covered with a mud dome.

WHEN ROBERT GLEN GIBSON of Cape Breton, Nova
Scotia, came home from his fishing trip on November 1,
1970, an awful lot of people had tuna fish salad. Gibson
landed the largest tuna ever caught—a leviathan
weighing 1,065 pounds!

A Pane-ful Story

Glass was made in prehistoric times, and glass-making
was already a well-established industry in Egypt by the
16th century B.C. The Romans refined the art of
glassmaking to a level unequaled until modern times.
They made small windowpanes, hollow ware, and
colorful millefiori (thousand flowers) vessels.

After the Crusades, Venice was the leader in
making fine glassware for almost four centuries. The
city officials tried to monopolize the industry by strictly
controlling the glassworkers at Murano. Artisans were
severely penalized for betraying the secrets of their art.

France became dominant in the 18th century with
the invention of a process for casting glass. French plate
glass was used to line the magnificent Galerie des
Glaces at Versailles.

The first glass manufactory on this side of the
Atlantic was built in 1608.

YOUR BIRTHDAY MAY NOT be such a special day after all—
you share it with at least nine million others.

THERE ARE 30 times as many people buried in the earth
as there are people now living.

AUSTRALIAN ABORIGINES are not in the least ashamed of their nakedness, and don't mind defecating in view of others. But they are quite embarrassed to be seen eating. Think of the problems such mores could create in one of our crowded cities!

Fancy Felines

"Ligers and tigons" may sound like a classic Spoonerism, but creatures of these names actually exist. They are the hybrid offspring of one of the rarest crossmatings of all—between a lion and a tiger. There are fewer than a dozen of these creatures in captivity today. When the father is a lion, the cub is called a liger; when the sire is a tiger, the animal is a tigon.

THE ELEPHANT IS the only animal with four knees.

A LITTLE-KNOWN INVENTION by Thomas A. Edison is a doll that talked, the first ever to do so. Built in 1888, the doll had a small phonograph in its body that enabled it to recite a dozen nursery rhymes. After making several hundreds of these dolls, Edison was informed that his company had previously sold the right to manufacture phonograph toys to another firm. Although that firm had never exercised its right, Edison stopped production and had the dolls destroyed. Of the few he saved and presented to friends, only two are believed to be in existence today.

OF THE ALMOST 4 billion people in the world today, approximately a third eat with a knife and fork, a third with chopsticks, and a third with their fingers.

ONE OF THE MOST spectacular homing-pigeon flights of all time took place in 1931, when a bird that had been taken from its home in Saigon was released in Arras, France, and found its way over completely unfamiliar territory to its Far-Eastern home. The bird made the trip in just 24 days.

As ANY TAILOR knows, in about 85 percent of men the left testicle hangs lower than the right.

DIVORCE, MOSLEM STYLE: According to the laws of Islam, a Moslem husband can divorce any of his four lawful wives by simply saying "I divorce you" three times. Wives do not have the same privilege.

Nicotine Nostalgia

Originally, tobacco derived almost exclusively from Turkey. American cigarette manufacturing dates from the Civil War period. During that era, Greek and Turkish tobacconists in New York City hand-rolled the expensive tobaccos then popular among the carriage trade: Havana, Turkish, Perique, Cavendish, Persian, Cut Navy, Latakia, and St. James. By the 1880's, natural leaf cigarettes, such as Bull Durham, began to dominate the market. The hoi polloi could buy a pack of smokes for a nickel.

Fatima, Sweet Caporal, Vanity Fair, Between the Acts, Melachrino, Murad, Wings, Spud—do these names ring a bell? Well, some of them are still around, but most of them are only nostalgic memories to veteran smokers.

JUST IN CASE you were wondering—the first Eskimo Bible was printed in Copenhagen in 1744.

ONE INCH OF RAIN contains the same amount of water as a ten-inch snowstorm.

IF THE EARTH were reduced to the size and weight of a ping-pong ball, and the sun shrunk accordingly, Old Sol would still be over 12 feet in diameter and weigh 6,000 pounds. And the sun is one of the smaller stars in our galaxy.

Magnificent Microcosm

Franklin H. Avers of Portage, Wisconsin, made a miniature electric village, which enacts the activities of an average midwestern town from late afternoon to sunrise. This model is mounted on a 5' by 12' stage. As the five-foot curtain opens on the scene, a breeze wafts the scent of flowers out toward the audience and flutters a flag in the park. A motorboat passes a sailboat on the lake, an automobile drives up to a house and honks its horn, and a plane glides in and lands noisily. The sun becomes reddish and finally disappears behind the mountain. Cattle moo, cowbells jingle, the moon appears, stars twinkle. A train pulls into the station, and all is still for a moment to signal the passing of several hours. The day begins to break, a rooster on a fence crows, the flag is raised, a plane roars, the curtain closes, and the five-minute performance is over.

SEVENTEEN HARVEST MICE have a combined weight close to that of a 150-pound man. The mice, however, need about 17 times as much food a day as does the man.

A FRENCH MAGAZINE conducted a survey to investigate sexual behavior in France. If the responses of those interviewed are to be believed, the average Frenchman sleeps with 11.8 women in his life, while the average Frenchwoman shares her bed with only 1.8 men.

THE SALTIEST LAKE in the world is the Dead Sea, which is so full of chemicals that it is really difficult for anyone to drown, or even remain fully submerged in it for any length of time. The chemicals make the water so heavy that it is also hard to swim. Each stroke you take makes you feel as if you're pushing away a ton of bricks. Of course, it's so easy to float in the Dead Sea that the thing to do is to get out there under an umbrella, hold a book in hand and simply lie on your back and read in comfort. But when you get out of the water, you'll find yourself covered with an oily film which is rather difficult to remove.

A BABY RATTLESNAKE at birth has the same amount of poisonous venom as a full-grown rattler.

WHAT COULD BE DRIER than a desert? Answer: The town of Arica, on the border between Chile and Peru. With a population of 14,000 inhabitants, Arica receives a mere .02 inches of rain per year. This is all the more remarkable because Arica is situated on the Pacific Ocean. To give you an idea of how dry this town is, the rainfall of Arizona—the driest of the 50 American states—is almost 400 times as heavy.

THE FASTEST BIRD alive is called—appropriately enough—the swift. This speedster is capable of speeds of more than 200 miles per hour.

FOUR MEN IN THE HISTORY of boxing have been knocked out in only 11 seconds of the first round.

THE FATTEST MAN who ever lived, Robert Earl Hughes of Fish Hook, Illinois, weighed 1,069 pounds in the last year of his life. Hughes' waist measurement at that time was 124 inches. When he died in 1958, he was buried in a coffin made from a piano case and transported to the cemstery by a moving van.

YOU'VE CERTAINLY HEARD of the 4-H Club, but did you know what the four H's stand for? Head, Heart, Health, and Hands.

THE HUMMINGBIRD IS the only bird that can fly backwards or hover in the same spot like a helicopter.

A Dubious Honor

In April of 1972, a little-known world title was lost at Beaver, Oklahoma. Governor David Hall of that state, who a year earlier had hurled a hand-sized wad of cow dung a whopping 94 feet to win the World Dung-Throwing Championship, managed a throw of only 68 feet and was dethroned by former Governor Dewey Bartlett, who broke all records with a stunning toss of 138 feet.

A TINY TROPICAL FISH called the anableps has eyes that work just like a pair of bifocals. The upper half of each eye is focused for water-surface vision, the lower half for underwater sight.

Captain Allardyce Barclay of Ury, Scotland, once walked 1,000 miles in 1,000 hours to settle a bet.

In the Book of Esther, it is stated that when the candidates for the Persian queenship were assembled by King Ahasuerus, they were brought to the royal harem and there treated for "six months with balm and six months with spices."

A Bevy of Terms

The English language was once rich with collective nouns to designate groups of animals. The most colorful terms, some of which are still in use, include: a *cete* of badgers; a *muster* of peacocks; an *exaltation* of larks; a *mute* of hounds; a *nye* of pheasants; a *skein* of ducks; a *pride* of lions; and a *skulk* of foxes.

THE GEODESIC DOME is the only man-made object that becomes structurally stronger as it increases in size.

THE WORLD'S RECORD for non-stop see-sawing is 101 hours, set by two California boys in 1964.

The Greatest Gladiator

In ancient days, rulers of Greece and Rome amused themselves and their subjects with gladiatorial contests of incredible brutality. One such sport, enjoyed by Greek monarchs, ordained that two men be strapped on a flat stone facing each other, almost nose to nose, with their fists encased in leather thongs studded with sharp metal spikes. At a given signal the two contestants would strike at each other, and the fight would continue until one contestant had been beaten to death. One of the greatest Greek gladiators, a strongman named Theogenes, faced 1,425 men in this life-or-death contest, and killed every one of them.

A CHAMELEON'S TONGUE is as long as its body.

THE NETHERLANDS—about 13,000 square miles in area—uses as much fertilizer in a year as the whole of South America, which has an area of almost 7 million square miles.

Posers

Why do we enjoy puzzles? What's the fun in being stumped, frustrated, maddened? Maybe it's man's love of a challenge, and maybe it's mere masochism. In either case, a good puzzle is hard to resist.

Perhaps the oldest of all puzzles is the riddle, and perhaps the most famous of all riddles is that asked by the Sphinx:

What goes on four legs in the morning,
on two at noon, and on three at night?

Oedipus answered the riddle correctly, and thus became Oedipus Rex. His solution: "Man. In infancy he crawls; in his prime, he walks; and in old age, he leans on a staff."

Another famous riddle is one that is reputed to have stumped Homer. Someone propounded these two lines to the bard:

What we caught we threw away;
What we couldn't catch, we kept.

The answer to this one is fleas.

Another early puzzle which continues to perplex us in its various forms is the labyrinth, an intricate arrangement of chambers and passages designed to befuddle the unfortunate person trying to navigate it. The great labyrinth of ancient times was built by Amenemhet IV of Egypt near Lake Moeris; its purpose is unknown. More renowned was a labyrinth built, according to Greek myth, in Crete by Daedalus to house the voracious minotaur.

In comparison, a crossword puzzle or jigsaw may

seem pretty tame. But anyone who has been stuck on a real toughie knows what a victim of King Minos must have felt like as he winded his way through the cul-de-sacs of the labyrinth, heading toward his death.

THE STATE WITH the youngest legal marriage age is New Hampshire, which permits a female with parental consent to marry at 13. Five states—Alabama, New York, South Carolina, Texas, and Utah—permit a female to marry at age 14. The youngest age at which a male may marry is 14, permissable only in New Hampshire.

THE LONGEST CHESS MATCH on record took place in Baku, U.S.S.R., in 1945. The match—which ended in a draw—took 21 1/2 hours and consisted of 171 moves.

WHEN YOU'RE STUCK on a crowded highway it may seem as if everyone and his brother owned a car. Actually, more than half of the people in the world still rely on their own or their animals' muscles for not only transportation, but all their other power as well.

OF ALL SYMBOLS appearing on the flags of the worlds, the star is by far the most common. Forty-one flags have this symbol in one form or another. The second most popular symbol, the crescent, appears on only nine flags.

ONE OSTRICH—the largest bird now living—weighs as much as 48,000 bee hummingbirds, the smallest birds in the world.

THE LARGEST MUSHROOM FARM in the world is located near West Winfield, Pennsylvania, in an old limestone mine. The farm produces about 14 million pounds of mushrooms each year.

THE TERM "limited" when used to refer to an express train does not, as often supposed, refer to the limited number of stops the express will make. Instead, it originates from the practice of running special fast trains with limited seating space.

WHEN THE WRIGHT BROTHERS made aviation history at Kitty Hawk, North Carolina, their initial 12-second flight spanned a distance shorter than the wingspan of a Boeing 747 jumbo jet—which measures 195.7 feet from tip to tip.

IT IS COMMONLY THOUGHT that an intestinal parasite, like a tapeworm, produces an insatiable appetite in its host. Actually, the amount of food necessary to maintain a parasite of this type is almost infinitesimal.

PLATINUM IS so malleable that a troy ounce of the metal can be stretched into a wire more than 10,000 miles long

THE MOST POPULAR BREED in the U.S. today is the poodle. In 1971, the American Kennel Club had 256,491 poodles on register. Compare this to 111,355 German Shepherds, the next most popular breed.

THE MOST SPECTACULAR musical event in the United
States occurred at the World Peace Jubilee, held in
Boston from June 17 to July 4, 1872, to celebrate the end
of the Franco-Prussian War. An orchestra of 2,000
instruments, including a bass drum 25 feet in diameter,
was bolstered by a chorus of 20,000. To lead this vast
aggregation in a rendition of *The Beautiful Danube*, its
composer, Johann Strauss, was brought from Vienna at
a cost of $20,000—and in 1872, that was quite a sum.

America's Favorite Hymns

Of the estimated 400,000 Christian hymns that have
been published, fewer than 500 are in common use, and
only 150 of them are well known by churchgoers. To
determine their popularity in this country, a poll was
made, not long ago, which disclosed that four hymns
alone constituted the first choice of 20,384 of the 30,000
churchgoers questioned. And the relative popularity of
these four outstanding favorites is shown by the
following figures: For every 100 persons whose first
choice was *Abide With Me*, the hymn that led, 75
preferred *Nearer My God to Thee*, 57 preferred *Lead,
Kindly Light* and 47 preferred *Rock of Ages*.

FISH CAN BE CAUGHT in the Sahara Desert. Strangely
enough, there are many underground streams in the
Sahara where, by digging through the sand, a desert
angler can obtain fresh-water fish.

THE U.S. ARMY OVERLAND TRAIN, the longest vehicle in the world, is 572 feet long—almost 1/10 of a mile! The truck, which is used to transport rockets or other very long objects, weighs 450 tons, has 54 wheels, 4 engines, and a 7,828-gallon fuel capacity.

THOUGH A STILT-WALKER isn't very speedy, he does get a unique perspective on the world around—and under—him. Hop pickers commonly go about their business on 15-foot stilts, but Albert Yelding ("Harry Sloan") of Great Britain mastered the art of walking on stilts that measured 22 feet from his ankles to the ground.

THE LONGEST RECORDED DRIVE of a badminton bird is 79 feet, 8 1/2 inches, achieved by Frank Rugani in California on February 29, 1964.

BIRMINGHAM, ENGLAND—an inland city—has more miles of canals than Venice, the "Queen of the Seas."

THE FLYING SQUIRREL does not have wings, and strictly speaking it cannot fly but only glide from tree to tree. No mammal except the bat is capable of true flight.

Top Dog

The greatest racing dog in history was Mick the Miller, a greyhound owned by an Irish priest named Father Brophy. Mick flashed sensational speed on the English tracks, and the Father was offered $4,000 for the beast. He accepted on condition that he receive the Derby purse if the dog won the classic. The Miller came through, winning $50,000.

In his three-year career on English soil, Mick never lost a race.

THE RECORD FOR cornhusking is 46.71 bushels in 80 minutes, set by Irving Bauman in 1940.

THE FIRST MUNICIPAL fire department in the United States was organized in 1659 by Peter Stuyvesant, governor of New Amsterdam. Stuyvesant distributed 250 leather buckets and a supply of hooks and ladders to his firemen and levied a tax of one guilder per chimney to maintain the department. The fire alarm was sounded by the twirling of a rattle, giving the department the nickname of "Rattle Watch."

Casting Lots

The dice game of Craps was introduced to America in 1813 by Bernard de Mandeville, who had seen a variation of the game played in France. De Mandeville brought the game to New Orleans, where it became popular among the Creole population. The nickname for a Creole was "Johnny Crapaud," and thus the game became known as "Crapaud's game," later shortened to "Craps."

De Mandeville himself was not lucky in the game, however, and was forced to sell a good deal of his property in New Orleans to pay his gambling debts.

TOMMY WOODS, WORKING for his college's radio station in Wayne, New Jersey, disc-jockeyed for 272 hours without a break in 1972—that's 11 full days!

OF ALL COMMON FOWL, the duck is the bird that requires the longest cooking.

A CAMEL CAN go without water for almost a week, and without food for much longer.

A PERSON WITH ordinary vision can distinguish about 150 different colors. An expertly trained eye can distinguish more than 100,000 colors, tints, and shades.

THE WORLD'S LARGEST ship model—a reproduction of the whaling bark *Lagoda* on exhibit at the Bourne Whaling Museum in New Bedford, Massachusetts—is three-quarters the size of the *Santa Maria* in which Columbus first sailed to America.

THE MOST POPULAR adult sport in Britain is dart-throwing.

BLOODHOUNDS CAN DETECT a scent up to 10 days old.

A STATUE IN THE PLAZA of Guayaquil, Ecuador, bears the name of José Olmedo, that nation's most famous poet. But the figure is actually a representation of Lord Byron, bought by the Ecuadorians in a London junk shop to save money.

Just Desserts

The first commercially made ice cream in the U.S. was sold by a Mr. Hall in New York City in 1786. The first ice cream soda was reputedly concocted by a Robert Green of Philadelphia, who, in 1874, added ice cream to plain soda water. But credit for the first ice cream cone goes to a young ice cream salesman at the 1904 Louisiana Purchase Exposition in St. Louis—or rather, to his date. The salesman, Charles E. Menches, gave an ice cream sandwich and a bouquet of flowers to the young lady he was escorting, and she rolled one of the layers of the sandwich into a cone to hold the flowers, thus founding an American institution.

GASOLINE HAS NO definite freezing point. Ordinary gas will solidify only under temperatures of between 180 and 240 degrees below zero—a temperature which has never been reached on this planet outside the laboratory.

BRUSSELS' BEST-KNOWN STATUE is "le Manikin Pis," a 20-inch figure of a boy responding to Nature's call, that has stood in the heart of the city for 500 years. During this time, personages such as Louis XV and Napoleon have presented the bronze lad with many medals, swords, and fancy uniforms which he has worn on appropriate occasions. Among the costumes have been the dress of a Belgian Grenadier, a French Chevalier, a British Master of Hounds, a Chinese Manchu, an Indian Chief, and an American G.I.

POPCORN IS ACTUALLY an Indian invention. The first Americans to enjoy popcorn were the colonists who attended the first Thanksgiving dinner, on Feb. 22, 1630.

DURING A LIFETIME the average human heart beats 2½ billion times.

THE LONGEST POEM ever penned by one man is the *Shah Namah*, written by the Persian poet Firdausi in the 10th century. The poem, known as "The Book of Kings," is 2,804 pages long, and its 120,000 lines fill nine good-sized volumes. Firdausi worked on the poem for 35 years.

THE CIVILIZED NATION with the longest average life expectancy is Sweden—71.6 years for men, 75.4 years for women. These figures just about match those of the Australian Aborigines.

THERE ARE MORE THAN 3,000 varieties of tea. Like wines, teas take their names from the districts where they are grown, such as Darjeeling, Assam, Ceylon, etc.

If at First You Don't Succeed . . .
The bridge that spans the Narrows Strait near Tacoma, Washington, is actually the second bridge built on that spot in the last 25 years. A 2,800-foot suspension bridge constructed there in 1940 blew apart in gale winds a few months after completion.

ONE OF THE EARLIEST recorded rail excursions was an 1840's day trip from London to Cornwall to view the public hangings in Bodmin jail.

DUE TO THE SHOWER of meteoric material, chiefly dust, falling from the sky, the weight of the earth increases by about 100,000 pounds each year.

THE LONGEST GOLF HOLE in the world is the 17th hole at the Black Mountain Golf Club in North Carolina. It measures 745 yards, and is a par 6.

The Millionaire Racehorse

The greatest racehorse in American history was undoubtedly Man o' War. Bought at auction for $5,000 in 1918, the phenomenal speedster went on to win 20 of the 21 races in which he was entered, earning close to $2,000,000 in purses and stud fees. So certain was Man o' War's victory that on some occasions the odds in his favor approached 1-to-100!

In addition to his race-course earnings, the remarkable stud sired 383 sons and daughters, who won a total of $3,500,000 in purses.

Man o' War was the first animal whose obituary and biography appeared in the list of celebrities compiled by the major press associations. The horse also had the largest personal guest book on record, with the names of 2,000,000 people who visited him in retirement. When Man o' War died in 1947, his funeral was attended by 2,500 admirers.

THE APOLLONICON WAS a gigantic instrument which could be made to sound like a symphony orchestra. First played publicly in London in 1817, the Apollonicon was played automatically or manually. The brilliant arrangement of its five keyboards enabled five persons to play a composition together.

IN 1965, A New Zealand resident produced the longest loaf of bread ever baked—20 feet, 5 inches long. The loaf weighed 50 pounds.

THE LARGEST CIGAR ever made—now on display in the Bunde Tobacco and Cigar Museum in Germany—is 170 centimeters (about 67 inches) long and 67 centimeters in circumference. The giant cigar would take about 600 hours to smoke.

THE HINDUS OF INDIA are said to play more varieties of musical instruments than are found in all other countries combined. The Hindus have several thousand instruments, for virtually all of their early instruments remain in use. In fact, their most popular instrument is still the seven-stringed vina, which was invented more than 1,200 years ago.

IN OCTOBER, 1957, Mrs. Beverly Nina Avery, a 48-year-old barmaid from Los Angeles, obtained her 16th divorce, thus becoming the most married-and-divorced person in the world. Mrs. Avery reported that five of her former husbands had broken her nose.

THE LOVEABLE KOALA BEAR is a finicky eater. He'll touch nothing but eucalyptus leaves.

A WELSH RABBIT has nothing to do with bunnies. It's a dish made with cheese and beer.

Faster Than a Speeding Bullet

A movie camera has been developed for taking pictures of objects traveling at extremely high speeds. If the camera—which takes 11,000,000 pictures a second—photographed a bullet traveling at the speed of 1,900 miles per hour, three minutes of normal-speed projection would be required to show just one foot of the bullet's travel.

SODA WATER WAS invented by a Philadelphia resident, Townsend Speakman, in 1807. He later added fruit juices to make the water more palatable.

PORTUGUESE EXPLORERS JOURNEYING to South America brought along convicts on their ships, who were cast ashore in unfamiliar areas to discover if the local natives were cannibals.

THE FROG FISH catches its prey with a built-in rod and reel. Strands of thin fleshy material are rooted to the top of the fish's head, and these dangling strands attract smaller fish—who are quickly gobbled up by the frog fish.

THE GABOON VIPER has the longest fangs of any snake. The specimen kept in the Philadelphia Zoo in 1963 was a little careless and bit itself to death.

A Trick Up His Sleeve

Why do men have buttons on their coat sleeves? Well, there's no functional reason for their existence, only a historic one. Frederick the Great of Prussia was greatly put out by the grimy sleeves of his soldiers' uniforms. He inquired why the sleeves were so much dirtier than the rest of the uniform, and was told that the soldiers were in the habit of wiping the perspiration on their faces on their sleeves. To stop the practice, Frederick ordered that buttons be put on the top side of all army men's sleeves. The unmindful soldier would receive a nasty scratch on his face the next time he used his sleeve as a towel.

Eventually, the buttons found their way onto civilian sleeves—but on the lower side of the sleeve. Today, to be in vogue, men must make the weighty decision of whether to adorn their sleeves with one, two, three, or four buttons.

The Dry Liquid

Liquid and *wet* are virtually synonymous, but in fact not all liquids are wet. At room temperature, mercury runs like water and changes its shape according to the container in which it is placed, making it a bona fide liquid. But mercury will not wet your fingers when you touch it.

THE SOCIAL WEAVER BIRD of Africa really deserves its name. As many as 90 couples may join to build a huge community nest. A favorite location is a big acacia tree. After the nest is built, each pair of weavers goes to work fashioning its own individual chamber inside the large structure—a bird version of the modern apartment house.

SAFFRON, FROM SPAIN, enjoys the distinction of being far and away the world's costliest spice. Its average import price in the U.S., between 1967 and 1968, exceeded $100.00 per pound, while Portuguese rosemary and Canadian mustard seed have been the least expensive of all spices and herbs. Between 1967 and 1968, the price for these last two has averaged somewhere between 7¢ and 8¢ per pound.

THE RECORD FOR non-stop Charleston dancing is 22½ hours, set by 23-year-old John Giola in 1926. But what's that compared to the record set by 35-year-old Cathie Connelly in 1969? Cathie did the twist for 101 consecutive hours—more than four days!

Word Play

Is a *skilligolete* something you might cook in, or a bacteria that causes a common disease? Would you buy *calibogus* in the lumberyard, or in a department store? Even if you're a crossword puzzle aficionado, these unusual English words may have you stumped. The answer to both questions is: neither. *Skilligolete* is a kind of soup, although you'd probably never come across any, as it's given mainly to sailors or prisoners; *calibogus* is a concoction made of spruce beer and rum.

Want some more? What's a *quockerwodger?* A *jobbernowl? Rumblegumption?* (Answers: a puppet; a dunce; a Scottish word for common sense.)

THE LONGEST AND HEAVIEST of all snakes is the anaconda of South America. Specimens have been reliably reported to be as heavy as 950 pounds, and as long as 37½ feet.

THE LONGEST SHADOW on earth is believed to be the one cast by El Pitron Peak on Tenerife, one of the Canary Islands. The mountain rises 12,200 feet above the Atlantic Ocean, and at sunrise and sunset casts a shadow nearly 150 miles long.

MERCURY, THE PLANET closest to the sun, is thought by most people to be extremely hot. Actually, at all times half of the planet is extraordinarily cold, with temperatures in the neighborhood of –250 degrees. The side of Mercury facing the sun, however, is broiling hot—temperatures there approach 700 degrees.

One Type of Speedster

The record for rapid typing is held by Albert Tagora of Paterson, New Jersey, who on October 23, 1923, typed an average of 147 words a minute for one full hour. During that stretch Tagora ran off 8,840 words—for an average of 12½ strokes per second!

THE LONGEST SERMON on record was delivered by a minister in West Richland, Washington, in 1955. The declamation lasted 48 hours and 18 minutes. A congregation of eight was still present at the sermon's end.

THE WORD *bride* is derived from an ancient Teutonic word meaning "to cook."

The Niftiest Natator

When Johnny Weissmuller retired from amateur competition in 1929, he could have taught Tarzan himself how to swim.

The handsome swimmer won his first National Championship in 1921. From then on, Johnny made records in every free-style distance from 100 yards to 880 yards and even held the world's record for the 150-yard backstroke.

His mark of 51 seconds flat for the 100 yards stayed on the record books for 17 years!

THE FACE IS sometimes dubbed the *mug* owing to the 18th-century practice of carving grotesque human faces on the outside of drinking mugs.

Sic Transit Records

Helene Madison held 16 swimming records at one time. At the end of 1932, the 6-foot, 18-year-old blonde from Seattle, Washington, held every important free-style swimming record. She had smothered all Olympic competition.

She was the first woman to swim 100 yards in one minute flat. Tank experts predicted that her records would last for generations. Today not a single one of Helene's marks stands.

THE WORLD'S LARGEST RODENT is the capybara, also called the carpincho or water hog. A native of tropical South America, it can attain a length of 3½ to 4½ feet and a weight of 150 pounds.

THE RECORD FOR non-stop piano playing is 44 days, set by Heinz Arntz in 1967. Except for two hours of sleep each day, the 67-year-old Arntz played continually for 1,056 hours. During his stint, which began in Germany, Arntz was carried in a van to a seaport and traveled from Germany to the United States on a steamship, finishing his performance at Roosevelt, Long Island.

Red Light, Green Light

You may think that the familiar red-green traffic signal is a product of the automotive age, but in fact the world's first traffic signal was installed outside the British Houses of Parliament, London, in 1868—decades before the invention of the automobile. With two semaphore arms—like the railroad signal of the day—and red and green gas lamps for use at night, the device was employed to ensure the safe passage of pedestrians across a busy intersection. Unfortunately, the signal blew up after a short period of use, killing a policeman.

The modern traffic light did not appear until 1914, when a red-green signal was installed on Euclid Avenue, Cleveland.

DOROTHY PARKER named her parrot Onan because the bird spilled its seed upon the ground.

THE LONGEST NATIONAL ANTHEM is that of Greece, which contains 158 verses. The shortest are those of Japan, Jordan, and San Marino, each of which contains but four lines. And the anthems of Bahrain and Qatar contain no words at all.

A Carload of Firsts

Gottlieb Daimler, a compatriot of Carl Benz, independently arrived at his own version of the internal-combustion engine that Benz had developed. Although the two never met, the firms which succeeded their enterprises merged and formed the present Mercedes-Benz company.

Perhaps the first truly practical gasoline-powered automobile was the Panhard, designed, in 1894, by a Frenchman named Krebs. The French had begun to produce autos a few years earlier, after Levassor purchased the French rights to Daimler's engine of 1887.

In the United States, several inventors get high marks for pioneering efforts in the field. Among them were the Duryea brothers, who won the first automobile race in America in 1895. One year earlier, an American named Elwood Haynes had gained the patent for a gasoline-powered car that was developed at the Apperson wagon works in Kokomo, Indiana. The first car manufactured in Detroit was made by Charles King in 1896. By 1898, there were no fewer than 50 automobile manufacturers in the U.S.

Which Way Is It to "Where Am I"?

When Spanish explorers first reached the Yucatan Peninsula in Mexico and asked the Indians what their homeland was called, they were answered with the word "Yucatan." The Spaniards then promptly gave the peninsula the name it bears today. But what does the word actually mean? Not understanding the explorers' question, the Indians had merely responded: *"Yucatan"*—"What do you want?"

ICED TEA WAS invented in St. Louis, Missouri, at the World's Fair of 1904.

A HONEYBEE CAN carry a burden 300 times its own weight. To equal this feat a 250-pound man would have to carry a 35-ton truck on his back.

CONTRARY TO ALMOST everyone's belief, the Pilgrims did not land at Plymouth Rock when they first arrived in America. The *Mayflower* first touched land at the tip of Cape Cod on November 11, 1620, and did not reach Plymouth Rock until the following December 21. The legend of the Pilgrims and Plymouth Rock originated in the 1740's.

A LAW IN SIENA, Italy, forbids a woman named Mary to work as a prostitute.

In One End, Out the Other

Each day the average person consumes, in one form or another, about three quarts of water. This liquid is released in urine at the rate of about 1/40 ounce per minute, for a total output of 1½ quarts of urine a day.

ALTHOUGH THE WHALE weighs over a hundred tons and the mouse tips the scales at only a few ounces, they develop from eggs of approximately the same size.

YOU PROBABLY KNOW that a female fox is a *vixen*, and a female peacock is a *peahen*, but how about a female aviator? She's called an *aviatrix*. And a female sultan is a *sultana*, a female maharaja is a *maharanee*, a female kaiser is a *kaiserin*, and a female cob (swan) is a *pen*.

A CERTAIN CEYLONESE INSECT so resembles a leaf that the creature is impossible to detect in a tree. The insect not only looks like a leaf in shape and coloration, but also sways in the wind to imitate perfectly the movements of wind-shaken leaves.

THE TUSKS OF some male African elephants eventually become so heavy that their owners must frequently rest them in the forks of trees. The longest African elephant tusk on record was some 11 feet long.

TABLE KNIVES ARE a rather late innovation. Until about 1600, diners brought to the table their own knives, which between meals served as daggers.

THE STATUE OF LIBERTY in New York City was paid for by donations from French citizens. American donations paid only for the concrete pedestal of the statue.

IF ALL SPACE between atomic particles were eliminated, matter in the resultant state—called the neutron state— would be so dense that one cubic inch would weigh about 1,800 million tons.

High Spirits

It was Louis Pasteur's research in the 1850's into the actions of yeasts and molds that resulted in the development of controlled fermentation that makes for a consistently good alcoholic product.

Freshly distilled spirits are stored in wooden casks for a minimum of two years to age and mature, during which time the bite of the tannin is lost. In the United States, spirits are aged at 103 proof (51½% alcohol); in Scotland, the alcoholic content is 124 proof (62% alcohol). Cognac is aged to 140 proof pure, which means 70% alcohol.

The casks in which the spirits are stored are made of American white oak; but French cognac is aged in Limousin oak and black oak. The casks are then stored in draft-free surroundings.

HAVE YOU EVER tried to figure out what bodies of water the expression *seven seas* refers to? Don't waste your time. The *seven seas* is a figurative term meaning all the waters of the earth. The expression appears in the ancient literature of the Hindus, Chinese, and Persians as well as in Western cultures.

THE 18TH-CENTURY Italian Cardinal Mezzofanti spoke 53 languages fluently, another 61 tongues almost as well, and understood 72 more dialects, for a total of 186 languages and dialects. Yet the Cardinal never left Italy in his entire life.

The Whiskerino Club

In 1922, when the city of Sacramento wanted to arrange a celebration commemorating the swashbuckling era of the forty-niners, they passed an ordinance compelling "all male citizens over the age of consent to grow whiskers and thus make the town look like it used to." Loyalty to their fair and sentimental city won over gallantry toward their wives and sweethearts; and all and sundry males became so enthusiastic over the idea, they even formed a Whiskerino Club, offering a prize for the longest pair of whiskers. A natty gent, sporting passementerie some 17 feet in length, won the first prize. In keeping with the whole idea, and feeling quite hellish, the Sacramento Club also awarded a prize for "the most impressive cootie garage." There are no further statistics.

WHEN IN 1608, Thomas Coryat, an Englishman who had visited Italy, introduced the Italian custom of eating with a dinner fork, everyone thought the idea was an insult to human dignity. But little by little, of course, this affront became standard practice.

Pile-up in the Atlantic

On May 27, 1945, the waters off Newfoundland must
have looked something like a Dodg'em-car course. On
that date, a convoy of 76 Allied vessels was steaming
through a dense fog when one struck an iceberg. The
remaining ships swerved sharply to avoid the berg, and
22 ships collided with one another within ten minutes.
Surprisingly, none of the ships was sunk, and no lives
were lost in the massive smash-up.

THE SPANISH OWE the name of their nation to the
Carthaginians of the sixth century, who gave the land
the romantic name of *Spania*, or "land of rabbits."

THE RECORD FOR the most consecutive sit-ups is held by
Wayne E. Rollins, who on September 13, 1971, did a
total of 17,000 sit-ups in 7 hours, 27 minutes.

THE FIRST RAILROAD STATION in the United States was the Baltimore & Ohio Railroad depot in Baltimore, Maryland. The two-story building, erected in 1830, still stands.

Packing Them In

The World Championship Sardine Packing Contest is held every year in Rockland, Maine. To pack a sardine, one must pick it up, deftly snip off its head and tail with razor-sharp scissors, and place it neatly in an open sardine can. The all-time record for sardine-packing is held by Mrs. Patricia Havener of Waldoboro, Maine, who in 1971 packed 450 sardines into 90 cans in just 10 minutes.

DOGS HAVE BEEN KNOWN to have litters as large as 23.

ENGLISH CONTAINS MORE WORDS than any other language—800,000—but it is doubtful that any individual uses more than 60,000.

A Shocking Tale

When attacking another fish, an electric eel can produce a current of 550 volts—more than four times the current produced by one electric wall outlet. The eel's current is produced by some 8,000 minute storage cells situated along the whole length of its body. The current runs between the eel's head, which is positive in charge, and its tail, which is negative.

Because the eel's vital nervous and swimming organs are electrically insulated by fatty tissue, an eel cannot electrocute another of its species.

CHOCOLATE FOR EATING was not perfected until 1876. M. D. Peter of Switzerland turned the trick. Today, Swiss milk chocolate is universally renowned for its flavor, color, and texture. But the most popular eating chocolate in the world is the plain old Hershey Bar, produced in Hershey, Pennsylvania, in the world's largest chocolate factory. The Hershey Factory turns out well over 200 million candy bars a year.

THE LONGEST SECTION of straight railroad track in the world stretches across the Nullarbor Plain in Australia. For 328 miles this track does not take the slightest curve.

TALK ABOUT YOUR fat cats! The heaviest domestic cat was a feline named Gigi who weighed 42 pounds.

FROM THE 11,200-FOOT peak of Mount Izaru in Costa Rica, you can see both the Atlantic and Pacific Oceans. This is the only point in the Americas from which such a view is possible.

The Straight and Narrow

The Green Lantern in Amsterdam bills itself as the "narrowest restaurant in the world." Its frontage measures just over four feet, and nowhere inside is the inn more than 20 feet wide. Nevertheless, the Green Lantern can accommodate 85 guests.

The narrow frontage is a relic of the times when an Amsterdam homeowner was taxed according to the width of his facade, which prompted the Dutch to build their houses as narrow as possible.

A MASSIVE MOSAIC in the Roman Catholic National Shrine in Washington, D.C. called *The Immaculate Conception*, stands 10 feet high and contains 35,000 pieces of stone. The selecting and inlaying of the stone required 25 man-years of labor.

A HEAVY DEW is actually the portent of good weather. On cloudless nights the earth loses its heat more rapidly, and a heavier dew results.

Steam Takes the Cake

Believe it or not, the first automobile race ever held was won by a car that was powered by a steam engine. On June 22, 1894, Paris was bubbling with excitement as 20 horseless carriages lined up for the 80-mile race from Paris to Rouen and back again to the big town.

Could these new-fangled things run at all? And if they did, would they prove as fleet and as durable as a few changes of horses?

Less than five hours later, a De Dion Bouton lumbered down the boulevards of gay Paree. The steamer had covered the distance at the dare-devil rate of 17 miles per hour.

THE BRITISH EAT one large loaf of bread each a week; the French and Germans, 1½ large loaves; and the Italians, 2¼ each a week.

THE INCA INDIANS, who built a massive empire in South America before Columbus sailed for the New World, did not have an alphabet or a written language.

SEALS SOMETIMES SWIM 6,000 miles over a period of eight months without once touching land.

IN 1949, THE HAIR of Swami Pandarasannadhi of India was reported to be 26 feet in length—the longest human hair on record.

The Bigger They Come, the Harder They Fall

Although only one foot long, a sea creature known as the urchin fish is capable of killing a 20-foot shark. The urchin fish is often attacked and swallowed by a shark. But once in the belly of the larger fish, the urchin fish blows up its prickly body like an inflated balloon, finally ripping apart the shark's belly and swimming out of the monster's body.

YOU'VE OFTEN WONDERED who holds the record for tobacco-juice spitting, right? Well, that noble distinction belongs to one Don Snyder, of Eupora, Mississippi, who in 1970 spit a wad of tobacco juice a whopping 25 feet, 10 inches.

Masterstroke

Out at the Inverness Golf Club in Toledo, they still call the seventh hole "Ted Ray's Hole." It is so named in honor of the great Britisher who won the U. S. Open there in 1920.

The hole itself is a 320-yard dogleg which can be straightened out to 290 yards—*if* you carry the forest between the tee and the cup.

Four times in the U.S. Open, Ted Ray cleared those woods: twice, he got directly on the green; once, he landed in a trap beside the green; and once, he came to rest on the fairway at the edge of the green.

The British pro scored four birdie 3's at this tough hole—and he won the championship by a single stroke!

IN 1952, THE FIRST TRAIN to run without motormen or conductors was placed into service in New York City, between Times Square and Grand Central Station. Nevertheless, a motorman was present in the car— although he did not perform any duties—because of labor demands by the Transit Workers' Union.

AN OTTER IS quick enough to dodge a rifle bullet.

THE MOVIE *Sleep* by Andy Warhol, the longest non-talking film ever made, consists solely of a man sleeping for eight hours.

The Long and the Short of It

The longest name of any city or town in the world belongs to the Welsh city of Llanfairpwllgwynggyl-lgogerychwyrndrobwell-Llantysiliogogogoch. Compare that to the French village of Y, or the Norwegian town Å.

THE AVERAGE ENGLISHMAN enjoys 2,000 cups of tea each year—that's almost six cups per day!

THE AUSTRALIAN WALKING FISH occasionally leaves the water and climbs a tree to enjoy a snack of insects.

AMONG THE UNUSUAL names for money throughout the world are: *Rupee* (India); *Cruzeiro* (Brazil); *Kyat* (Burma); *Balboa* (Panama); *Quetzal* (Guatemala); *Bolivar* (Venezuela); *Sucre* (Ecuador); *Gourde* (Haiti); and *Zloty* (Poland).

Southpaws, Take Heart

Many theories have been advanced to explain the dominance of right-handedness. One of these theories holds that the origin of this phenomenon is physiological, the result of an unequal distribution of the viscera in the abdominal cavity. A more commonly accepted view, however, is that right-handedness is primarily a product of primitive warfare. Early man was engaged in a continual struggle for survival with his fellow man. When called upon to protect himself and his family, he would instinctively protect the vital region around his heart by fending off blows with his left arm, while using his right to strike blows against his adversary. Through a long process of natural selection, those men who had powerful right arms survived to pass their hereditary characteristics on. The natural southpaws who were forced to battle with their right arms fell by the wayside.

THE GATEWAY TO the fortress of Purandhar near Poona, India, is built on a foundation of solid gold. The 50,000 gold bricks in the foundation would be worth over $40 million at today's prices.

THERE IS ENOUGH STONE in the Great Pyramid of Cheops, in Egypt, to build a wall around all of France. The construction of the massive tomb required the work of 100,000 men for 20 to 30 years.

Gustatory Gymnastics

The next time you're thinking about setting a record, try your hand at one of the following gastronomic achievements. The records for consuming various items are:

Raw eggs: 56 in 2 minutes
Potato chips: 30 bags in 29 minutes
Sausages: 17 in 90 seconds
Oysters: 480 in 60 minutes
Prunes: 100 in 12 minutes
Beer: 2½ pints in 10 seconds

Bon appetit!

THERE IS ONLY one case on record of a country being moved from one continent to another—at least on maps. Before Panama gained its independence from Colombia in 1903, the nation was considered a part of South America. After independence, the Isthmus was regarded as a part of Central America—which belongs to North America.

ON THE AVERAGE, a city dog lives longer than a country dog—11 years compared to eight.

THE STUPIDEST CREATURE ever to inhabit the earth was the *Stegosaurus*, a six and one-half ton creature with a brain weighing only two and one-half ounces.

IF THE AIR-CONDITIONING were turned off in the Houston Astrodome, the entrance of warm humid air could cause it to rain in the stadium.

THE FIRST AIR-CONDITIONED office building in the United States was the Milam building in San Antonio, Texas, which was completed in 1928. The 21-story structure was the first office building in the world to be built with air-conditioning as a part of the original construction.

On October 7, 1965, 16-year-old Charles Linster set a record for push-ups that will be hard to beat. Performing for three hours and 54 minutes, Linster executed 6,006 push-ups without stopping.

If you're ever hightailing it from a bear in the woods, don't try the old trick of climbing a tree to escape. Almost all bears can climb trees.

Stand-ins

An old Chinese law permitted a substitute to die for a convicted murderer. A condemned man with enough money could often find a replacement to suffer decapitation for him, with the payment going to the substitute's family.

OVER 65 PERCENT of the world's population goes through the day without coming in contact with a newspaper, radio, television, or telephone.

Highway Favorites

What's the most popular make of American car? Well, if we take the 1971 figures, it's the Chevrolet, with 2,320,777 in sales.

The next most favored car is the Ford, with 1,761,112 cars sold.

A distant third is the Oldsmobile, which sold 775,199 cars.

THE MOST POISONOUS SUBSTANCE yet discovered is the toxin of the *Clostridium botulinum* bacteria. Just 1/3000 of an ounce of this toxin could poison the entire human population of the earth.

IF THE ENTIRE population of the earth were crammed within the boundaries of the United States, the population density of our nation would still not reach that of Belgium or the Netherlands.

WHEN THE HEADMASTER of a high school in Oregon began broadcasting the names of absent students every morning on the radio, truancy at his school dropped by 25 percent.

THE FIRST FERRIS wheel was erected at the 1893 Columbian Exposition in Chicago. Built by George Ferris, the wheel had 36 cars, each capable of holding 60 passengers, and rose to a height of 264 feet.

Parting Ways

There are over 35 different legal grounds for divorce in the United States, but not one of these grounds is legal in all 50 states. A loathsome disease can result in a divorce in Kentucky and Illinois. Joining a religious sect which does not believe in marriage provides sufficient grounds in Kentucky and New Hampshire. But attempting to take the life of a spouse is grounds for divorce only in Tennessee and Illinois, and intolerable severity, only in Vermont. And in Virginia, the guilty party in a divorce granted on the grounds of adultery cannot remarry without the consent of the court.

ANTEOJOS IS THE Spanish word for eyeglasses. Anteojos comes from two Spanish words. *Ante* means "in front of" and *ojos* means "eyes." So *ante ojos* means "in front of the eyes," which is exactly where eyeglasses belong.

JEAN FRANÇOIS GRANDET, a stuntman who performed under the name of Blondin, once walked over a tightrope strung across Niagara Falls—while wheeling a wheelbarrow! On another occasion, Blondin walked across the Falls blindfolded.

ON A CLEAR DAY, you can see forever from a lookout point near Chattanooga, Tennessee. Seven states are visible from this promontory—Tennessee, Alabama, Georgia, South Carolina, North Carolina, Virginia, and Kentucky.

SCIENTISTS IN THE ANTARCTIC region are often amazed to find king penguins who—apparently even more amazed by the men—keel over backwards in surprise.

The Twain Meets

Owing to the twist of the Isthmus of Panama, the Atlantic Ocean is, in some places on the Isthmus, actually west of the Pacific. Thus, there is a point in North America at which the sun rises in the Pacific and sets in the Atlantic. In fact, a boat in the Panama Canal runs northwest to southeast in passing from the Atlantic to the Pacific.

A 23-FOOT IRON PILLAR in Delhi has not rusted in 1,500 years—and no one has figured out why.

To Golf or Not to Golf

"It looketh like a silly game," quoth King James IV of Scotland in 1491, signing a law that prohibited the playing of golf. "I'll not have our brave boys beating up the pasture with a stick when they could be out a-practicing with the trusty bow-and-arrow!"

"Why do ye not try it yourself, sire?" queried a crafty courier.

"Aye," said the King. "I'll do that. But only to show ye that it be a silly game."

"If Your Majesty would borrow my sticks . . . " volunteered another.

And that's why the law of 1491 was repealed. But you can be sure that the Scots would have continued to play their game, law or no law. Golf is the national game of Scotland, and no land has ever had a fiercer devotion to a sport.

Since the mid-15th century, golf has enjoyed great popularity in Scotland, but the origins of the game probably go back much further in time. The word "golf" is commonly supposed to be an adaptation of the Dutch word *kolf* ("club"), but this is highly uncertain, for there is no record of the Dutch having played a game analogous to the Scots' golf.

WILLIAM H. HARRISON enjoyed the shortest tenure of all American presidents. Harrison died barely a month after taking office in 1841, allegedly from the strain of an arduous campaign, and was succeeded by John Tyler.

Idols of the King

When King Farouk fled Egypt in 1952, a number of personal items were left behind in the monarch's luxurious palace, among them: a vast collection of American comic books; 50 walking sticks; a pocket radiation counter; 75 pairs of binoculars; 1,000 ties; a set of photographs depicting copulating elephants; an immense stamp collection; and a $20 double eagle which had vanished some years before from the Philadelphia Mint museum.

THOMAS HARIOT, AN English mathematician sent to the colonies by Sir Walter Raleigh, is the first Englishman to have smoked tobacco, but his patron became the most famous smoker of Renaissance England. Raleigh acquired the taste readily, and became a passionate devotee. It is recorded that Raleigh even "tooke a pipe of tobacco a little before he went to the scaffolde."

THE EARLIEST MENTION of an inn is found in Aristophanes' *The Frogs*. In the play, a group of men enter an old tavern, where they devour 16 loaves of bread, 20 meat balls, garlic, fish, and cheese, and then make off without paying the bill.

THE RICHNESS OF the English language and its genius for particularization are well demonstrated by a look at those words used to identify young animals. For instance, a young frog is called a polliwog; a young swan, a cygnet; a young hen, a pullet; a young oyster, a set; a young goose, a gosling; and a young swine, a shoat.

THREE MEN HAVE BEEN ELECTED to the American Presidency with less popular votes than one of their opponents: John Quincy Adams in 1824, Rutherford B. Hays in 1876, and Benjamin Harrison in 1888. In addition, 12 other men have been elected President without a majority of the popular vote. The last was Richard Nixon, who in 1968 won only 43 percent of the popular vote.

WHEN THE POPULATION of lemmings in the Scandinavian mountains grows too large, the mouse-like creatures swarm down over the plains and plunge headlong into the sea, where they swim until they sink to their doom. This is the only instance of periodical mass suicide among mammals.

Monkey Business

A Southern psychologist installed two chimpanzees in adjoining cages, and tried to determine how quickly they could distinguish between two different-colored coins. One cage contained a slot machine that dispensed water only after the insertion of a white coin; the other cage contained a machine that dispensed food and worked only with a black coin. On the first day, each chimp was given a bagful of mixed coins, and soon learned which coins worked his machine.

A few days later, the chimp with the water dispenser was deprived of water for 24 hours, and the one with the food dispenser was deprived of food for 24 hours. Then the thirsty monkey was given food coins, and the hungry one water coins. Instead of being baffled by the ploy, the chimps reached through the bars of their cages and exchanged coins with each other.

THE PLANET VENUS takes 247 earth days to spin around on its axis, and 224.7 earth days to orbit the sun. Thus, the Venusian day is longer than the Venusian year.

Surprisingly enough, Jupiter—the largest planet in our solar system—has the shortest day. The massive planet requires only 9 hours and 50 minutes to make a complete rotation on its axis.

THE GREBE, THE MUTE SWAN, some ducks, and the loon have a special way of caring for their young. Very often, especially at the first sign of danger, the crested grebe sinks until its back is level with the surface of the water. Its young climb onto its back. Then the parent grebe rises to its swimming position, and with strong strokes carries them across the water to safety.

THE WORLD'S RECORD for chin-ups is 78, set by Anton Lewis in 1913. And the record for one-handed chin-ups, 27, was set by a 38-year-old woman, Lillian Leitzel, in 1918.

THE MOST BALLS a juggler has successfully kept in the air at one time is 10, a feat accomplished by Enrico Rastelli in 1920.

OKOLEHAO, AN EXOTIC Hawaiian alcoholic beverage, is made out of molasses, Koji rice, and the juice of the Kalo plant.

As Old As the Hills

Perhaps the oldest living thing on Earth is the Macrozamia tree, which grows in the Tambourine Mountains of Queensland, Australia. Scientists estimate that these trees are anywhere from 12,000 to 15,000 years old—more than six times as old as the giant redwoods of California and Oregon.

Although there is some controversy over the exact age of these palmlike trees—counting their concentric rings is a very difficult task—everyone agrees that the Macrozamia is unequaled in age. The giant bald cypress of Mexico is definitely known to be 4,000 years old, and is far younger than many of the Australian Macrozamias. These treees were old when David and Goliath were boys.

THE GREATEST LOG-ROLLING exhibition ever recorded took place in 1900 in Ashland, Wisconsin. Two lumberjacks, Alan Stewart and Joe Oliver, spun a log for three hours and 15 minutes without tumbling into the water.

THE FIRST SIDEWALK in the United States was laid in 1657 on a New York thoroughfare called—what else?— Stone Street.

THE ANIMAL THAT takes the longest time to make its debut is the elephant. Its gestation period is 645 days or more than 21 months.

THE HINDU TEMPLE of Siva at Madura, India, is adorned with an estimated 1 million intricately-molded idols, although legend claims that there are more than 30 million idols on the temple. To count them alone would take years.

The Three-Mile Landscape
The largest painting ever painted was the mammoth "Panorama of the Mississippi," completed by John Banvard in 1846. This painting depicted the 1,200 miles of river scenery from the mouth of the Missouri to the estuary of New Orleans. For people to see the 12-foot-high and nearly 16,000-foot-long picture, the mammoth canvas had to be passed between two upright revolving cylinders on the stage of a large auditorium.

It took a spectator two hours to see the painting in its entirety.

METEOROLOGISTS ESTIMATE THAT if all the sparks produced by all the dynamos in the United States were fused together, the result would be but a half-sized lightning flash.

A TRAIN DOESN'T TIP OVER when going around a curve because the rail on the outside of the curve is higher than the rail on the inside of the curve.

GOPHERS LOVE TO EAT the lead sheath around telephone cables, thereby disrupting transcontinental service.

The Noon Watch

In 1642, Rembrandt painted "The Shooting Company of Captain Frans Banning Cocq," in which 29 life-sized civic guards are shown leaving their armory at high noon, with the sun shining brightly upon them.

Less than 200 years later, the picture had become so dingy and dark that someone facetiously called it "The Night Watch," a nickname that has since supplanted its true title.

THE WORLD'S MOST COMPLETE collection of sheet music belongs to the Edwin A. Fleisher Music Collection in Philadelphia. More than 12,000 compositions from nearly 60 countries are included.

AN ADULT AFRICAN elephant needs 300 lb. to 400 lb. of fodder a day.

TEN STATES IN ALL have been named after people: Louisiana, Virginia, West Virginia, Maryland, New York, Pennsylvania, Georgia, Washington, North Carolina, and South Carolina.

Four state capitals are named after presidents: Jackson, Mississippi; Lincoln, Nebraska; Jefferson City, Missouri; and Madison, Wisconsin.

THE DEEPEST LAKE in the world is Lake Baykal, in the Soviet Union. At some points it is more than a mile deep.

ALTHOUGH THE ROMANS took baths and had excellent plumbing facilities for hot and cold water more than 2,000 years ago, the habit of bathing died out during the Middle Ages. Baths were usually taken only on a doctor's request. The result was a lack of hygiene that encouraged infection. Even the United States did not get its first bathtub until 1840.

THE UNITED STATES is by far the world's largest importer of spices and herbs. In 1968, this country imported over 150 million pounds of spices, with a value in excess of $60 million.

TODAY, THE CUSTOM of the Mussulman is to carry a comb with him to manicure his whiskers. He does so immediately after prayer, while still on his knees, and any strands of hay that fall out of his beard are carefully picked up and preserved for burial with the owner. Five hundred million Mohammedans still swear by the beard of the Prophet.

Good Things Come in Small Packages

Mrs. Pemberton, a 16th-century painting by Hans Holbein, brought $30,000 in a 1935 auction. The round portrait is only two inches in diameter.

THE EGYPTIAN QUEEN Cleopatra was Greek by ancestry and had not a drop of Egyptian blood in her veins. The famed Queen of the Nile was descended from a line of brother-sister marriages, and she herself married two of her own brothers.

IN 1960, THE *Journal of the American Medical Association* reported that a patient checking into a hospital for a swollen ankle had been found to have swallowed 258 items—including a 3-pound piece of metal, 26 keys, 39 nail files, and 88 assorted coins.

FLAVORED SPIRITS, INCLUDING GIN, aquavit, absinthe, and zubrovka, are produced by redistilling alcohol with a flavoring agent. Juniper is used to flavor gin; caraway seeds, to flavor aquavit.

THE FIRST RECORD of the use of spices dates from the age of the pyramids in Egypt—approximately 4,600 years ago. Onions and garlic were fed to the 100,000 laborers who toiled in the construction work under Cheops. These vegetables were administered as medicinal herbs to preserve the health of the laborers.

Playing Possum

When in mortal danger, many animals feign death. But none do this as convincingly as the American opossum and the dingo, a wild dog of Australia. The dingo will allow its captor to beat it unmercifully until the chance to escape presents itself. The entrapped opossum will assume its famous "possum" pose, which is to lie limp with its tongue hanging out of its mouth and its eyes open and rolled back.

EVEN TODAY, the British eat almost eight ounces of sweets per person per week, more than any other people.

One-Wheel Antics

In 1934, a vaudeville performer named Walter Nilsson pedaled across the United States on an eight and one-half foot high unicycle—and never once fell from the bike. Nilsson completed the 3,306-mile trek in just 117 days.

Incidentally, Steve McPeak of Tacoma, Washington, rode a 32-foot unicycle in 1967. That must be a record!

IN CASE YOU'VE FORGOTTEN: the face of Woodrow Wilson adorns the U. S. Treasury's $100,000 note. And, of course, Salmon Portland Chase appears on the $10,000 bill.

Teamwork

The *Panthéon de la Guerre*, a gigantic panorama of the first World War completed in 1918, was the work of 130 individual artists, probably the largest number of artists to work on a single picture. The mammoth work—402 feet long and 45 feet high—contains battlefields, flags, monuments, and the life-sized portraits of 6,000 war heroes.

AMSTERDAM POLICE HAVE a special branch, called the *grachtenvissers*, whose only duty is to cope with motorists who drive into the canals.

THE RECORD DISTANCE for spitting a watermelon seed is 38 feet, 8¾ inches, achieved by Lee Roberts of Rio, Wisconsin, in 1972.

THE TIME REQUIRED for the earth to orbit the sun—that is, the length of an earth year—increases by about .04 seconds each century.

GEORGIA, WITH AN area of 58,073 square miles, most nearly approaches the average size of the 48 conterminous states.

Dope on Diamonds

The largest diamond ever found was the 1½-pound Cullinan diamond, unearthed in South Africa in 1905. Other notable diamonds: the Koh-i-noor, now among the British crown jewels; the Hope diamond, the largest known blue in existence; the Star of Africa No. 1, cut from the Cullinan; the Tiffany, an orange-yellow diamond; and the Dresden, a greenish diamond.

The green variety of beryl is known as emerald; the blue is aquamarine. Highly prized in antiquity, the emerald was a particular favorite in pre-Columbian Mexico and Peru. An 11,000-carat emerald was reportedly found in South Africa in 1956.

Sapphire is a variety of transparent blue corundum. It is mined primarily in Asia and Australia, though some sapphires are to be found in Montana. The "Black Star Sapphire of Queensland" is the largest cut gem-quality sapphire.

OPINION DIFFERS ABOUT the moral value of coffee. Despite suppression on religious and political grounds, coffee became the universal beverage of Islam. It was then opposed by Italian churchmen as a drink of the infidel, but was Christianized by Pope Clement VIII. By 1650, coffee had reached most of Europe. Although introduced in North America about 20 years later, coffee became the staple American drink only after tea had been downgraded with the Boston Tea Party of 1773.

THERE IS ENOUGH STONE in the Great Wall of China to build an eight-foot wall around the earth at the equator.

THE MOST LONG-LIVED animal is the giant tortoise of the Galapagos Islands. Specimens have been estimated to be as old as 190 years.

A Spirited History

The use of liquor is so widespread that almost every country in the world utilizes some native product to make an alcoholic beverage. Asian liquors, distilled from rice, from millet, or from palm sap originated around 400 B.C., and took the names of *sautchoo, arrack, arika,* and *skhou.* Around the year 300, Ireland brewed up some *usquebaugh* from oat and barley beer. Around the year 900, Italy began distilling grapes to produce brandy. Around 1500, the Scots got the hang of making whiskey from malted barley. In 1750, France distilled cognac from grapes.

A PLAY BY Sinclair Lewis entitled *It Can't Happen Here* opened in 21 theatres in 18 cities—on the same night of Oct. 27, 1936.

KING RICHARD II of England was so careless with royal funds that the monarch once had to pawn his crown to make ends meet.

MAN HAS DEVISED some rather exotic ways to make a living, and in many cases has come up with equally exotic words to identify these professions. Here's a sampling of some less familiar terms: a *puffer* is an auction booster; an *abigail* is a lady's maid; a *boniface* is an innkeeper; a *couturier* is a dressmaker; a *tonsorialist* is a barber; a *factotum* is a jack-of-all-trades; a *grifter* is a circus concessionaire; a *costermonger* is a fruit peddler; and a *croupier* is a gambling-house employee.

THE TOUCAN'S BILL, which is bigger than its body, gives it an ungainly, comical appearance. But in spite of its large size, the thin-walled bill is lightweight and easy to carry.

THE FIRST NIGHT GAME in baseball history was played on June 2, 1883, at League Park in Fort Wayne, Indiana. The game pitted a boys club team against the Quincey professionals and was witnessed by 2,000 spectators. The field was illuminated by 17 lights of 4,000 candlepower each.

What a Doll

The Queen's Dolls' House, presented to Queen Mary of England in 1924, may be the world's most intricate miniature. Constructed on a scale of one inch to one foot, the house is almost nine feet long, five feet wide, and five feet high. It has more than 50 rooms, its own electric generator, a functioning elevator, a plumbing system, and a wine cellar with genuine cobwebs covering its minuscule bottles of real vintage wine. Its library contains hundreds of actual books, most of which were handwritten by such well-known authors as Kipling.

ON JUNE 13, 1948, a Los Angeles resident named Jack O'Leary caught a fit of hiccoughs. It was not until June 1, 1956—about 160 million hiccoughs later—that the fit ended. During that time, the unfortunate Mr. O'Leary lost 64 pounds, and received through the mail over 60,000 suggested cures for hiccoughs.

Livy relates that when the barbarians overran the Golden City, a Roman senator sat still, unmoved at everything, until a Goth touched his beard—then he struck, although he died for the blow.

There are about 98,000 postmen in Britain. Of these, 3,000 were bitten by dogs in 1968.

The crawling fish of Asia can live for a week out of water. In fact, this fish will instinctively leave a stream that is going dry and head for the nearest water, often traversing a mile or more of dry land.

Flight of Fancy

The world record for altitude by a model aircraft is 26,929 feet by Maynard L. Hill (U.S.) on September 6, 1970, using a radio-controlled model. The speed record is 213.71 m.p.h. by V. Goukoune and V. Myakinin with a motor piston radio-controlled model at Klementyeva, U.S.S.R. on September 21, 1971.

NICHOLAS JOSEPH CUGNOT of France is credited with the invention of the first automobile. Cugnot built himself a steam-powered tricycle in 1769 which attained a speed of 2 m.p.h. while carrying four people.

In a Nutshell

Early American artists were fond of miniature wood-carvings, but in some cases they may have carried their craft a bit too far. The Peabody Museum in Salem, Massachusetts, contains a wood carving done in the inside halves of a rosary bead which depicts, in one half, Judgement Day, and in the other, Heaven. The entire scene in each half is less than 2 cubic inches in area, yet includes close to 50 figures—none of which can be seen without a magnifying glass.

THE WILDCAT IS the most vicious fighter in the animal kingdom. Asleep, it resembles a gentle housecat—in a fight, it is a furry ball of rage. This spitfire's speed gives it an advantage over most other animals. In one swift leap, it can rip open its enemy's throat with its razor-like teeth.

THE TOBACCO PLANT was first brought to Europe for cultivation in 1558 by Francisco Fernandes, a physician whom Philip II had sent to the New World to report on its products. Jean Nicot, the French ambassador at Lisbon, sent some tobacco seeds to Catherine de Medici, queen of France, and was immortalized by the application of his name to tobacco's most baleful element, nicotine.

C. ARTHUR THOMPSON of Victoria, British Columbia, Canada, had played golf for many a year. It kept him so agile that he even was able to tour the links when he was past 100 years of age. On October 3, 1966, at the age of 97, he managed to shoot a round lower than his age. Thompson scored a 96 on the 6,215-yard Uplands course.

THE HIGHEST NUMBER with a name is the centillion, which is 10 with 600 zeroes, or 10^{600}.

NG KA PY is how you order a shot in Peking. It's made from millet, with various aromatics added.

IT IS ABOUT ten times as easy to shoot a hole-in-one in golf than it is to roll a perfect 300 game in bowling. The odds against the bowler are about 300,000 to 1, while the golfer "enjoys" odds of 30,000 to 1.

THE RUWANWELI PAGODA in Anuradhapura, Sri Lanka (Ceylon), is built on a 500-square-foot, seven-inch-thick foundation of solid silver.

Got a Match?

According to one theory, the superstition that "three on a match" is unlucky dates back to the days of trench warfare during World War I. Soldiers believed that by holding a match long enough to light three cigarettes, they were providing the enemy with enough time to aim his shot and perhaps bring down the unlucky matchholder.

FISH CAN GET seasick if kept on board a ship.

THE POINT OF zero degrees latitude and zero degrees longitude lies in the Gulf of Guinea off the western coast of Africa. The closest land to this point is in Ghana, and the capital of that nation—Accra—is the nearest town.

THE OLDEST ALCOHOLIC beverage we know of is mead, a wine made from honey. The sweet drink is stored in wooden casks, and must be left to mature for up to five years.

Mead is the national drink of Poland. The stiff attitude the Poles displayed while enjoying their mead prompted Napoleon to tell his troops to "drink, but in the Polish fashion."

THE LONGEST JAIL SENTENCE on record is 381 years, passed on a 16-year-old boy in Montreal in 1964. The youth had pleaded guilty to six counts of attempted murder and a series of armed robberies.

DURING THE CONSTRUCTION of the Hoover Dam, concrete had to be poured *continually* for two years.

NOT ALL INSECTS taste with their mouths. Insects such as the butterfly and house fly do have tongues for licking and sucking food, but they also carry taste organs on their feet which are especially sensitive to sugar.

Minutiae

The smallest flowering plants in the world are Wolffia and Wolffiella which make up the green film seen on fresh-water ponds. These flowering plants, known as the duckweed, run from one-thirtieth to one-fiftieth of an inch in diameter. The duckweed is but one seventy-millionth the size of the mammoth *Amorphophallus titanum,* the world's largest flower.

Index

Farouk, King, 207
father, youngest and oldest, 126
fattest man, 158
Fernandes, Francisco, 224
ferris wheel, first, 204
Ferris, George, 204
fertilizer, 161
Fessenden, Prof. Reginald
Aubrey, 56
"Fiesta of the Radishes," 105
Figueroa Street (Los Angeles),
25
filibuster, longest, 47
fingernails, 73
Firdausi, 173
fire department, first U.S., 169
firearm, 49, 58
First Construction in Metal, 86
fish, 15, 76, 51, 81, 159, 223
flying, 19
in Sahara, 166
largest caught, 51, 138, 152
smallest, 14
walking, 198
fishing, 45, 55, 114, 134-135,
138
Five Points (gang), 44
flag, 40, 164
flamingo, 39
flea, 14, 41, 162
Florida, 100
flower, smallest and largest, 227
food, consumption, 136, 200
footwear, 23, 46, 58, 80, 137
Ford, Henry, 12
fork, dinner, 190
Fort Wayne, Indiana, 222
fossil, 42
4-H Club, 158
France, 46, 107, 113, 144, 152,
154, 157
Franco-Prussian War, 166
Franklin, Benjamin, 28, 68
Frederick the Great, 178
frigate bird, 97

frog fish, 177
frog, 120
Frogs, The, 208
fruit tree, 43

Gaboon viper, 178
Galileo, 57
Gallegos, Don Jose, 75
gambling, 61
Garfield, James A., 87
gasoline, 171
gazelle, 91, 126
gem, 98, 105, 108, 128, 219
General Electric Co., 101
geodesic dome, 161
Georgia, 117, 219
German language, old, 43
Gettysburg Address, 94
geyser, 62
Gibraltar, Strait of, 96
Gibson, Robert Glen, 152
Giola, John, 180
gladiator, 161
Glasgow University, 79
glass, 133, 152
glider, longest flight, 89
golf, 46, 61, 104, 108, 132, 145,
174, 206, 225
courses, 56, 104, 108, 111,
174
gopher, 213
Graham, Sylvester, 52
Grand Canal (China), 21
Grandet, Jean François, 204
Grant, Lawrence, 79
grave digging, 73
Great Exhibition of 1851, 147
Great Salt Lake, 109
Great Wall of China, 117, 220
Greece, 137
Green Lantern, 194
Green, Robert, 171
Greenland, 34-35
greyhound, 46, 168
Guayaquil, Ecuador, 171

Lozier, 8
Luxembourg, 50
Lu-Yu, 36

Mace, 123
MacLennan, Dr. Munro, 79
Macmillan, Hector, 140
Macrozamia tree, 211
Madison, Dolly, 95
Madison, Helene, 183
Madison, James, 58, 95
Madura, India, 213
Mallon, Mary, 135
Malta, 116
Man o' War, 174
Manchuria, 58
Mandeville, Bernard de, 169
Manhattan, 8, 17
Manley, Norman L., 111
Maoris, 45
Marc, Jacques, 27
Marconi, Guglielmo, 22
Marcus, Siegfried, 121
Mariana Trench, 93
Marquis, Theresa, 35
Marrakesh, Morocco, 51
marriage age, legal, 163
marriage customs, 71, 114
Marriott, 100
Martinique, 131
Mary, Queen, 222
Masai tribe, 70
Matisse, Henri, 7
Maxwell, James Clark, 22
Mayflower, 187
McPeak, Steve, 217
mead, 227
measurement, systems of, 53,
  148
Medici, Catherine de, 224
Menches, Charles E., 171
mercury (element), 57, 179
Mercury (planet), 181
Mexico, 27, 100, 105, 122, 137
Mezzofanti, Cardinal, 190

Miami, Florida, 97
Michelangelo, 35
micropantograph, 79
Mill Reef, 127
miniskirt, 30
Minos, King, 163
minotaur, 162
mirror, as weapon, 60
"Miserere," 88
Mississippi River, 17
Missouri, 61
models, 127, 156, 170, 223
molasses, 126
Moluccas, 10
monkey, 10, 67
Mont-St.-Michel, 107
Montana, 66
Montauk Point, New York, 51
Moore, Jimmy, 74
Morley, Christopher, 149
Morocco, 151
Mosconi, Willie, 74
Moscow, U.S.S.R., 44
mother, youngest and oldest,
  126
mound builder, 140
Mt. Everest, 93
Mt. Izaru, 194
Mt. McKinley, 129
Mt. Washington, 76
Mt. Whitney, 88
Mousetrap, The, 31
movie, first scented, 139
Mozart, W.A., 88
Mundus, Frank, 51
Munich, Germany, 63
murder rate, 50
Museum of Modern Art, 7
mushroom farm, 164
musical instruments, 18, 48, 54,
  63, 75, 86, 107, 130, 146,
  147, 166, 175, 176
musket, 49

Names
  feminine, 187

saffron, 179
Saga, Emperor, 67
Sahara Desert, 113, 145, 151,
    166
Saigon, Vietnam, 154
St. Bernard, 144
St. John the Divine, Cathedral
    of, 92
St. Louis, Missouri, 17, 26, 62,
    171, 186
St. Patrick, 116
St. Peter's Church, 35, 41
Salem, Massachusetts, 224
saluki, 46
Samuelson, George, 144
San Antonio, Texas, 201
San Francisco, California, 67, 98
San Jose, California, 97
Sanctorius, 57
sans-culottes, 58
sardine, 15
sardine packing, 192
sarissa, 65
Scotland, 24, 56, 104
sea
    color of, 20
    creatures, 110
    "seven seas," 189
seal, 196
Sears, Roebuck Co., 32
Seattle, Washington, 97
see-sawing, 161
Sen, Mihir, 96
sentence, longest in literature,
    67
sentence, longest jail, 227
sermon, longest, 181
Seurat, Claude, 39
"seven seas," 189
shadow, longest, 180
Shah Namah, 173
shampoo, 47
shaving, 16, 66
    see also beard
sheet music collection, 214

Sheik of Araby, The, 107
Shen Nung, 36
shoe, see footwear
shrew, 111
Siam, 124
sidewalk, first U.S., 211
Siena, Italy, 187
Sigmund, John V., 62
silkworm moth, 8, 72
Sistine Chapel, 88
sit-ups, record non-stop, 191
skates, 13
Skegness Amusement Park, 94
skin, 127, 151
skinniest man, 39
skunk, 56
Slavs, 49
sleep, 118-119
Sleep, 198
Smith, Mrs. Emma, 94
snail, 67
snake, 116, 178
snow, 35, 66, 107, 139, 156
Snow White, 12
Snyder, Don, 197
soap, 141
soda water, 177
Soleure, Switzerland, 47
song title, longest, 26
South Africa, 136
Spain, 40, 50, 110, 179, 191
Speakman, Townsend, 177
speech, longest, 47
spice, 10, 94, 149, 160, 179,
    215, 217
spitting, 70
spoonerism, 153
Springer, Phillip, 26
squirrel, flying, 168
Sri Lanka, 80, 96, 102, 226
star, 112, 156
Statue of Liberty, 188
Stegosaurus, 201
Stevens, Thomas, 67
Stewart, Alan, 211

stilts, 167
Stonehenge, England, 86
Strauss, Johann, 166
street, longest, 25
Stuyvesant, Peter, 169
sun, 156
superstitions and customs, 71,
    78, 114, 226
Supreme Court, 134
surname, most common, 33
Sussex, England, 30
Sutoku, 7
Swami Pandarasannadhi, 196
Sweden, 173
sweets, consumption of, 217
swift, 158
swimming, 62, 64, 96, 109, 157,
    182, 183
Syracuse, Sicily, 60

Tacoma, Washington, 173
Taft, William H., 82, 122
Tagora, Albert, 181
Taj Mahal, 63
Tanzania, 70
tapeworm, 165
tapioca, 82
tarot card, 84
Taylor, Anna Edson, 140
Taylor, Mrs. Zachary, 95
tea, 67, 102-103, 173, 128, 133,
    142, 198
    discovery of, 36
    smuggling, 77
    transport of, 71
teeth, decorating, 132
telephone, 125
telescope, largest, 130
temperature, lowest recorded,
    138
Tenerife, Canary Islands, 180
Tennessee, 61
tequila, 137
termite, 82

tern, 79
testicle, 155
Theogenes, 161
thermometer, 57
Thieme, Johann Heinrich Karl,
    73
Thompson, C. Arthur, 225
thunderstorm, 19
tides, 103
tiger, 153
tigon, 153
Titanic, 126
tobacco, 31, 50, 65, 110, 155,
    207
    as legal tender, 26
    first European cultivation,
        224
    pipe, Chinese, 64
    pipe, Eskimo, 53
    use by women, 95
tobacco-juice spitting, 197
toci-toci beetle, 30
Tokyo Observatory, 107
toothache, 93
topaz, 105
tornado, 26
tortoise, 36, 220
toucan, 222
Tour d'Argent, 121
Tourcoing, France, 47
towns and villages, oddly-named,
    96
track & field, 109
traffic fatalities, 81, 106
traffic light, first, 184
Trans-Siberian Railroad, 44
trapping, 100
tree, oldest, 211
trial by touch, 83
tuna, 152
Turkey, 62, 136, 155
Twain, Mark, 142
typewriter, Hoang, 90
typhoid, 135
typing (speed), 181

Underpass, smallest, 8
unicycle riding, 217
U.S. Air Force Missile
 Development Center, 115
U.S. Army Overland Train, 167
U.S. National Safety Council, 59
U.S. Naval Research Laboratory,
 72
U.S. Open, 197
U.S. Patent Office, 80
University of Arizona, 45
urchin fish, 196
Uruguay, 143
Ury, Scotland, 160
Utah, 60, 105, 109

Vaughn, Theresa, 125
vehicles
 land sailboat, 30
 longest, 167
 marsh buggy, 72
 windmill wagon, 99
Venezuela, 13
Venice, Italy, 23, 71, 152, 168
Venus, 210
Venus space probe, 21
Vermillon, Ohio, 31
Versailles, France, 152
Victoria, Queen, 115
violin, 48
violinista, 48
Virginia, 26
vodka, 143
volcano, 27, 63, 108, 131

Waetzel, Karl, 146
Wagner Labor Relations Act,
 134
walking, long-distance, 62, 160
war, shortest, 146
Warhol, Andy, 198
Washington, D.C., 82, 118, 125,
 194
water
 consumption, 187

in earth's surface, 89
watermelon-seed spitting, 219
waves, highest, 106
Wayne, New Jersey, 169
weaponry, 58, 60, 65, 123
weaver bird, 179
"Weighing of the Mayor," 119
weight, heaviest lifted, 117
Weissmuller, Johnny, 182
Welsh rabbit, 177
West Richland, Washington, 181
West Winfield, Pennsylvania, 164
Westinghouse Co., 104
whale, 12, 70, 187
whipping, public, 82
whiskey, 81
White, Dave, 61
White House, 118
Whyos (gang), 44
wildcat, 224
Wilmer-Brown, Maisie, 31
Winchester Country Club, 61
wind velocity, 76
Wisconsin, 156
Witmark Publishing Co., 87
wives, exchange of, 71
Woods, Tommy, 169
World Dung-Throwing
 Championship, 159
World Peace Jubilee, 166
World's Fair, 104
worm, longest, 24
Wright Brothers, 165

Yangtze River, 21
Year Knife, 101
Yelding, Albert, 167
Yellow River, 21
Yellowstone National Park, 62
Yucatan Peninsula, 186

Zaharee, James W., 94
Zanzibar, 146